Creating a Home for Body, Soul, and Spirit

Creating a Home
for Body, Soul, and Spirit
A New Approach to Childcare

Bernadette Raichle

Waldorf Early Childhood Association of North America

Managing Editor: Lory Widmer
Copy Editing and Proofreading: Kristine Hunt and Jennifer Kleinbach
Photographs: Awhina Day Nursery and Kindergarten
Graphic Design: Sheila Harrington
WECAN Administrative Support: Melissa Lyons

The song "Wonder" on page 197 is printed by permission of Michael Winship.
© 1990 Michael Winship

© 2011, 2008 Waldorf Early Childhood Association of North America
Second English Edition
Published in the United States
by the Waldorf Early Childhood Association of North America
285 Hungry Hollow Road, Spring Valley, NY 10977

This publication is made possible through a grant
from the Waldorf Curriculum Fund.

ISBN: 978-1-936849-01-7

Table of Contents

Chapter 4
The Physical Sheath

Chapter 5
The Etheric Sheath

Chapter 6
The Soul or Astral Sheath

Chapter 7
The Ego Sheath

Part 2: Principles and Practices at Awhina

Chapter 8
Principles of Good Management

Chapter 9
The Role of the Co-Worker

Wonder

How like an Angel came I down!
How Bright are all Things here!
When first among his Works I did appear
Oh how their Glory did me Crown!
The World resembled his Eternitie
In which my Soul did Walk;
And every Thing that I did see
Did with me talk.

Thomas Traherne

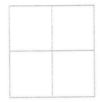

Acknowledgments

My thanks to the co-workers at Awhina, both past and present, who have each contributed to the development and growing of a worthy "home away from home" for the children of today.

Thanks to my main co-worker and husband, Gerrit, who so graciously "received" Awhina when I was unable to continue my full-time involvement in the day nursery. This enabled me to engage in the new work that I am doing today, bringing what has been developed at Awhina into the world. I thank him for his constant support in proofreading and for his major contribution to nutrition, meals, and recipes.

Cynthia Aldinger and I first met in Australia in 1993 at a Vital Years Conference where she was keynote speaker. Since this first meeting, it became apparent that we shared a mutual concern for childcare and an aspiration to create "care" environments that both support and enhance the path of development into life for infants and young children. I sincerely thank Cynthia for her colleagueship, for making time in her extraordinarily busy schedule to read the original manuscript, and for her heartwarming Foreword.

It was Marjorie Thatcher who first made my work known in North America after visiting Awhina in 1990. As colleagues in the world, we share a common interest and concern for modern family life and in particular the incarnating journey of the very young child. It is due to Marjorie's invitation that I am presently teaching in the West Coast Institute's Infant and Toddler Caregiver's Course in Vancouver. I thank Marjorie for giving her time to read and comment on the manuscript.

To Janet Meterlerkamp, a parent at Awhina for almost five years, I thank you for the Afterword, "A Mother's Story," told as only a mother can, from the heart.

To WECAN Publications Managing Editor, Lory Widmer, an artist in the true sense of the word, who has crafted my sometimes enigmatic manuscript into a book worthy of reading—my heartfelt thanks for your clarity and for your inspiring suggestions. ▣

— *Bernadette Raichle*

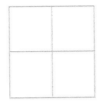

Foreword

Cynthia Aldinger

Looking like cherubs with shining faces full of innocence, two tiny children surprised me with their quiet appearance after naptime at the Awhina Day Nursery and Kindergarten. Having spent the whole morning there, I could hardly recall having seen these little ones earlier in the day. What had happened?

When they had awakened, their caregivers had helped them with toileting and washing up and then had given them a gentle face washing and oiling and a lovely hairbrushing. They were renewed for the rest of the day, and indeed appeared like "new" children to me! With smiling faces they invited me into their world, which at that point consisted of having an afternoon snack and playing outside in the garden.

As with everything that happens at Awhina, these children and their playmates had been met with loving care and penetrated practices meant to best support young children when they must be away from their own homes during the day. The foundation of these penetrated practices lies in a fourfold understanding of the human being, which can also be applied to the development of a home. This way of understanding the environment and activities of healthy home-life is what sets the unique tone and depth of anthroposophically-based child care. It is not just the doing of certain things, but also the understanding that surrounds and deepens the doing. The heart of this book is the description of this fourfoldness, both in the human being and in the environment of the home.

During my visit, I felt as if I was dropping in on a neighbor, though I was thousands of miles from my home! Yet, it did feel like I was in someone's home

—someone with many children. There were twelve children there, ranging in age from about seven months old to four or five years old, and three to four caregivers throughout the day. There was no feeling of "the old woman in the shoe who didn't know what to do" with so many children. Indeed, a feeling of family and "home" pervaded my experience.

This is how I first met Bernadette Raichle. Even though she was out of the country when I was there, I felt I was meeting her essence through her work, the creation of this center of care and devotion to young children. I was introduced to Awhina by another colleague, Marjorie Thatcher, who had visited Awhina several years earlier and had brought photographs back to our Waldorf Early Childhood Association Board meeting. This was near the beginning of my calling to become involved in the development of anthroposophically-based child care in North America, and when I saw the photographs I set myself the goal of seeing Awhina for myself!

When I was invited to speak at the Vital Years Waldorf Early Childhood Conference in Sydney, Australia in 2003, I determined to "stop by" New Zealand on my way. Days after being at Awhina, I met Bernadette at the conference in Sydney. A few years later I worked with others to bring her to North America to share her work with us.

Awhina, which will unfold before your mind's eye as you read this book, is a haven of care for young children and also, I daresay, for their parents. Imagine the comfort a parent experiences when leaving a child in a place that feels like dropping him off at grandma and grandpa's house. It does not have to do with the age of the caregivers, but with the mood that is expressed by the type of care provided.

I still remember when I walked through the front door and smelled the cooking smells in the kitchen. Several little ones were playing near the caregiver who was preparing the meals for the day. Other children were playing in the living room, which was cozily arranged like the living room of a home, while another caregiver ironed the play cloths and a third caregiver read a story to a couple of toddlers.

In another room a few slightly older children were deeply engaged in self-directed creative play, free of the hovering of an adult. The adults were fully aware of these children and did check up on them, but (as in a healthy home) there was no feeling that these children were in a "program" where this was the part of a "curriculum" set aside for creative play. They were just free to be. If there was a problem they knew where to go for help if necessary.

Back in the living room something else was happening. Apple time. One of the caregivers brought in from the kitchen a bowl of freshly cut-up apple slices, and I was enchanted as I watched the children gravitate to the bowl and stare off into infinity as they munched away. This was not morning snack, but a casual little pre-snack that came at just the right time for these growing little ones. It was like a healthy pause in the daily routine, and one could sense the deep breathing that it created. Soon thereafter came the more formal family-style snack at the table—one of the most beautiful tables I have seen.

The whole day unfolded in a similar fashion, breathing in and breathing out, with no rushing from one thing to the next—indeed, I felt there was all the time in the world.

While outside, I experienced the same level of penetrated practices that I had met inside the home. There were gardens to be tended, chickens to be fed, and even a few lawn chairs for sitting and relaxing while the children played. The outside area was the most artistically-designed play yard I have experienced. Sidewalks were not there just for getting from point A to point B—rather, they wound about and had magical stones and shells embedded in them. Seeing the garden gate was like receiving a beautiful invitation to a garden party. Passing through its portal, we left behind one magic

kingdom in order to enter into another. There were two or three small lawn statues placed in just the right proximity to a bush or tree—not too many, but just enough to support the enchantment.

These are not, however, formal English gardens as shown in fancy garden books. No, these are children's gardens, or what we in North America would call a nice backyard. And the children meet these gardens through a gradual progression from inside the house to outside in the largest play area. Upon first going outside, a well-designed covered deck supports the children in their preparation for being outside. When all are ready, the gate is lifted, and they move into the smaller play yard with a small sandbox just right for the littlest children. When I was there the chickens in their coop were also in this first play yard and waiting to be tended by the children and caregivers. Following the magic winding sidewalk we came to the garden gate that invited us into the larger play yard with the big sandbox and well-constructed, yet simple, play equipment. This included a wonderful rowboat, which took the children on great excursions. While the play equipment was enjoyed, equally appreciated were the bushes and trees and scattered tree stumps. There was enough variety of gradation and form that a child could easily feel either "hidden" or out in an open expanse.

When it was time to go inside, one child was given the privilege of watering down the sandbox—a very gentle spray that stipples the sand in order to discourage cats and also to give a fresh appearance to the sandbox for the next day. Staying outside with this child and one of the caregivers, I became the object of "play" when the child, brandishing the hose, began chasing me around the garden with squeals of delight. This little fellow gave me the feeling that I was experiencing a rite of passage, and was now a member of the Awhina family, a great aunt from across the ocean! What a privilege!

In Sally Jenkinson's book *The Genius of Play* she uses the term "Children's Culture" as being different from "School Culture." What I have been describing at the Awhina Day Nursery and Kindergarten is the former, and some would say that this culture of childhood is at risk. While many fun and engaging activities are available for children now, the self-created experience of just being a child at home is becoming less common. Creative childhood, bathed and surrounded by the practical and meaningful activities of focused adults leading "yes"-filled lives, is a foundation for creative adulthood.

Perhaps it is time for us to recognize that simplicity is profound. In an enigmatic way, we could even say that simplicity is complex! If we choose to examine what is happening when a young child is in an environment such as that provided at Awhina, we will actually find that whole worlds of experience are opening up for the child. And not just for the child, but for the adults as well. The inner harmony that is created through such strong rhythms and routines is the best health-giving prescription one could ask for in the "apothecary" of natural living. Bernadette has written about the framework built around the ongoing growth and development of the co-workers and also how a deep and warm relationship is fostered with the children's parents.

This framework again hearkens to the tending of the fourfold sheaths—the physical, the life body, the soul body, and the spirit—that require nurturing and heightened awareness in order to create such havens of healthy living. What Bernadette is offering in this book is not meant to be a template for creating replicas of the Awhina Day Nursery. Rather she is sharing the deep roots of how Anthroposophy informs the daily rhythms and rituals of caring for children. Anthroposophy offers to the world a deep wisdom of human development. In fact, translated it literally means "wisdom of the human being"—*anthropos* (human being) and *sophia* (wisdom). At the same time, Bernadette is offering a picture of how such wisdom informs healthy, practical and enlightened childcare practices.

Those of us who have chosen to dedicate our lives to caring for children and their families in our "home-away-from-home" settings can be grateful to Bernadette and her co-workers for setting such a fine example for us.   ▣

Cynthia Aldinger is the Executive Director of LifeWays North America and a Board Member of the Waldorf Early Childhood Association of North America. She teaches and lectures internationally.

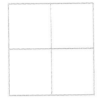

Introduction

I created this book for all who carry a deep interest for the growing child in their hearts. It has been written in an attempt to show Anthroposophy, founded by Rudolf Steiner, as something that can easily be used as a practical and supportive tool in our everyday lives in raising children. The word *Anthroposophy* comes from the Greek and simply means "wisdom of the human being." This book is meant for the student of Anthroposophy as well as for the caregiver, parent, or educator who is searching for and exploring new ways of caring for and educating the young child.

While the study of Anthroposophy is a lifelong path of personal development, I have endeavored, in this writing, to express the human, practical, day-to-day living aspects of this philosophy, which allow the reader to begin a relationship to something that can otherwise appear as rather mysterious and therefore intangible in what it has to offer. It is its relevance to everyday living through practical application that makes Anthroposophy so very accessible—particularly in today's world where the life of the family, and therefore the healthy development of the soul, spiritual, and physical nature of infants and young children, is so much at risk.

While my work with infants and young children in a care environment is based on an anthroposophical image of the human being, the practice and inspiration for this work have developed out of insights gained in more than twenty-five years of working with young children and their families. This work has brought with it challenges, for which I am grateful, and inspirations for which I feel blessed.

In writing this book I want to bring something new to the world of childcare. I want to show that there is another way to care for little children in an out-of-home environment, while at the same time maintaining the focus and importance of the home as being the heart in the life of the growing child.

There are many books that cover in greater depth such areas as child development, the development of movement, speech and language, and so on, and therefore it would be repetitive for me to write of something that has already been more than adequately covered by specialists. For this reason I include a list of suggested further reading in addition to the reference list of books cited in the text.

I would like to specifically acknowledge Veronica van Duin and her work, *Homemaking as a Social Art*. Her all-embracing image of the home as something living that needs to be cared for and its relevance in today's society brings a new-found purpose to the inspirational task of homemaking, while at the same time affirming my own imagination of the home and its importance in this world of busyness that surrounds the modern family.

Childcare has become more readily available in the past few decades, growing from something relatively small to a burgeoning "industry." It has become a product-oriented industry, which sees infants and young children cared for in group situations, usually defined by age and with as many as thirty children, sometimes more, in any one group. In New Zealand, childcare is strongly supported by a government that is encouraging—one could almost say *pressuring*—mothers back into the workforce, ostensibly for the good of the women and the country...but what about the children?

We are led to believe that these children are being well cared for. They have the latest equipment, they have space to "play," they are fed and their developmental needs are being addressed by well-trained staff who monitor their developmental milestones by keeping personal profiles. These children can be in such a center up to ten hours each day! Centers may be open all hours to suit parents' extraordinary working needs. The needs of parents today have changed, it seems but the important question that begs to be asked is: have the needs of infants and little children changed?

This is a book about childcare from a different perspective. It is about the life of the family, of which the child is an intrinsic part. The child cannot be separated off from the family when we discuss childcare. This book is about supporting the family of today by offering a form of childcare that both respects and emulates the home—a form of childcare that embraces nurturing practices of the home and family, and at the same time provides a role model for the parent.

Many young parents tell me that they feel "all at sea" when it comes to parenting and the creating of the home, along with juggling home and work expectations. The modern family today, with all its choices, needs support and nourishment as at no other time in history. Without this support, archetypal family life, which once served to surround the young child as a second skin, strengthening and preparing the child for the real world, will continue to erode. However, with appropriate support for the family there is the possibility to change something in society.

Manfred Schmidt-Brabant, lecturer and author, asks the questions: What is to become of the family? What is to become of the home, which has been the foundation of society for centuries? He states that the basis for human relationship is found in the home. When we speak of "culture" we can no longer refer to a large community. This is why the home has become the bearer of culture.[1]

We could say that the home is the foundation of society. As such it needs all the care and attention that we can offer, for it is the home that carries the possibility for the future that will uphold the values that enable society to maintain health. It is this underlying motif of the home, of caring for the child, of nurturing the family, that is the heart of anthroposophical childcare.

References made to Awhina Day Nursery and Kindergarten, co-directed by the author, simply serve as examples. This book is not about yet another "program" but about the fundamentals of anthroposophical childcare. ▣

— *Bernadette Raichle*
  Havelock North, New Zealand
  Whitsun, 2008

---

1   Manfred Schmidt-Brabant, *The Spiritual Task of the Homemaker*, 25.

The Origin of Awhina
Day Nursery and Kindergarten:
A Personal Journey

My story begins when my children entered the local Waldorf school. The first time I stepped into the school environment, I remember thinking, *This is what I want for my children.* What was it I felt?

I was a young mother finding my way and, like all parents, wanting the best for my children. This was in the early 1970s. New Zealand was still a country where wealth was fairly evenly distributed, and this created a feeling of contentment about life among New Zealanders. Life was good in New Zealand. Families were generally still intact. Mothers were very much at home with their children, at least in my social circle.

Family life was the focal point. My contemporaries and I breastfed our babies, shared kindergarten carpools, held coffee mornings, attended spinning groups and book clubs, and generally were engaged in all the tasks that caring for a home, family, and husband entailed. We were homemakers. We were busy and content with our lives. We were happy with what we had, which was actually very simple—and at the time one wage coming in to the home was adequate. Our fulfillment came from homemaking, which we engaged in with pride, and we were active in what we considered important issues in society as well.

We advocated for breastfeeding mothers to be able to nurse their babies when and where they wanted. We were staunch supporters of baby-led weaning. I vividly remember the day that I spoke on local radio, passionately expounding the benefits of breastfeeding and responding to callers as they rang in with their questions.

On another occasion I was asked by the sympathetic matron of our local maternity home if I would speak to the doctors and nurses about how to better support the breastfeeding mother. I was a breastfeeding counselor for La Leche League, and to this day I do not know how I mustered the courage to stand before a large group of professionals and tell them how it was done.

On another occasion action was required when the local hospital board threatened to name our new maternity home "the maternity unit." With babies in backpacks, a friend and I walked the streets gathering signatures to support the view that women having babies were not ill and should therefore not be treated as such. Our maternity home was just that—a home—and not a hospital ward as the name *unit* implied. Again, with babies on our backs, we presented our petition to the board, a rather staid group of elderly gentlemen. I don't believe the hospital board had had such a visitation before: two mothers with wriggling babies on their backs. The following night the decision was reported in the local newspaper. The new maternity home would be known as *Arohaina*, a word from the Maori meaning "loving nest,"—a name that the matron and staff had advocated for, but which had fallen on deaf ears.

And so homemaking was my focus, albeit brightly colored with a strong social conscience that was able to be freely exercised if and when the need arose.

During the early 1980s, I was part of an enthusiastic group of parents who established the first satellite Rudolf Steiner kindergarten in New Zealand, attached to and administered by the existing Steiner school but on a separate site. We found a beautiful old bungalow on a huge one-half-acre section of land. Those of us with kindergarten-age children felt strongly that for such young children to be traveling up to an hour in a car or bus each day was counterproductive. Ideally we would have loved to be able to walk our children to kindergarten. However, as I recall, even parents who lived relatively close to the kindergarten still arrived by car!

Our wish was that this kindergarten would truly become a kindergarten for the community, including the surrounding neighbors into our daily life and activities as much as possible. We did this by inviting them to and including them in all our festivals, fairs, and other events, whenever possible. This community kindergarten soon became an environment filled with life and activity.

During these early stages my involvement was that of a coordinator of parent activities and fundraising, including the making of eurythmy shoes for the school classes. The knowledge and life experience of older members of the anthroposophical community was acknowledged, and these people were invited to come and speak to the parent community to share their wealth of experience. Their talks were diverse and topics ranged from plants and herbs to home nursing hints, to name just two. We offered recorder lessons, formed a choir, and learned about the celebration of the festivals. The garden was large and quite overgrown when the property was purchased by the school, and so a group was formed to develop and maintain this green haven. Looking back I realize how fortunate I was to have been given such a wonderful opportunity in preparation for my future work.

From time to time I was invited into the children's realm. The kindergarten teacher at the time, who later became and is to this day my colleague, would invite me and my spinning wheel into the inner sanctum of the kindergarten room. There I would find a corner and spin! The children, mostly oblivious to me but unconsciously absorbed in the rhythm of the wheel, continued their often intensive "work" of play.

Here I experienced a whole new world of possibility for children. From a purely practical perspective I was able to experience children at play as I had never seen before. I had naturally seen the play of my own children, but with the eyes of a mother. This was observation from a totally objective viewpoint, and the very environment seemed to sing with the earnest intensity of play.

This led me to a major life decision: to go to the United Kingdom and train with Margret Meyerkort at the Wynstones Kindergarten Training in Gloucester. Although I had already worked in the kindergarten for two years (I had been asked to substitute at the Hastings Kindergarten), I was not someone who could assume this important work without gaining the necessary preparation. My three children would stay in New Zealand with their father, surrounded and cared for by their wonderful class teachers and some very good friends. During my study time in England, I experienced the life of the kindergarten in Germany and Portugal as well as England. Children may be brought up surrounded by their own unique culture, but no matter where they are in the world, they play as all children play, and the play itself is archetypal in its essence, though colored by what comes to them from their environment,.

On my return to New Zealand, I "officially" began my career path with children, with my friend and colleague. This career led me on a path of awakening and self-development that continues today.

During the late 1980s while at the Steiner kindergarten, my colleague and I would ponder over what we were offering the children. While their kindergarten morning was filled with rhythm and carefully prepared activities, the afternoon threatened to undo all that the morning had aspired to. For many children, afternoons were spent in the car, going to the supermarket, shopping, or other activities. We were also aware that our work reached only a small group of families with their children.

We would plan and dream about providing for the children in the afternoon, allowing for a nutritious lunch, a rest or sleep, and then home after an afternoon play or activity, in accord with the more mellow feel of the afternoon.

This remained a dream. The kindergarten was part of a long-established Steiner school with a long-established protocol. This was not the time to bring such sweeping changes.

However, a seed was sown, to lie dormant for some seven years until conditions allowed that seed to begin to germinate. This came about not in the way we had envisaged all those years ago, but in a way that was timely and allowed for a new way of being, a new form of working with very young children from an anthroposophical perspective that responded to the life of the modern family and the new needs that were beginning to unfold.

My colleague now worked for a government agency that offered advice and support to established and new daycare and early childhood facilities. During this period, she had the possibility to experience many different types of facilities and situations where babies, toddlers, and young children were being cared for. It was fast becoming apparent that the need for daycare for the very young child was not going to go away. Childcare was becoming a way of life for children and their families and would become even more so in the future.

I did not necessarily agree with how children were cared for in existing daycare facilities, but the people leading these facilities were in the main well-intentioned. I felt that standing in judgment of childcare as it was offered was not going to improve or change anything for children. If I wanted to create a change of thinking in the way children were cared for, then I needed to place myself in that environment and show that there was another way. Little children needed the protective environment that a home could offer. I felt strongly that there existed a need to provide a different type of care—one that acknowledged the qualities inherent in each of us and that supported the threefold elements of the body, soul, and spirit.

In New Zealand, diversity in the realm of early childhood has always been encouraged, and to provide a different way of caring for very young children allowed choices for parents that they otherwise would not have. This required a new paradigm of thinking from an anthroposophical perspective, and for some this was difficult. I could understand this reluctance on the one hand, for this was a completely new way of looking at the care of the young child as well as the emerging needs of families. However, on the other hand, I saw the reluctance as the result of a rather insular way of viewing the world, the rapidly changing ways of society, and the needs of the family.

Working with childcare from an anthroposophical perspective provides an opportunity to express a new approach to education in a way that at once becomes understandable to all because of its very practical application. I see anthroposophical childcare as a means of breaking down barriers that still exist today in relation to anthroposophical education.

I believe *home* in the true sense of the word is indeed the best place for children. However, the home of today is not the home of yesteryear—the world is a vastly different place to that of the 1980s and before. Parents of today need much greater support in their parenting and in the creating of their family culture. The anthroposophical day nursery, in its holistic approach to homemaking and the care of the young child, carries the potential to do just this.

In August 1993, Dr. Michaela Glöckler was the keynote speaker at a national anthroposophical conference that I attended in New Zealand. Her topic was the care of the senses in the young child. This dramatically confirmed my wish, which now I personally carried as a sense of responsibility, to provide a facility that acknowledged the physical, soul, and spiritual development of the very young child at the most crucial and vulnerable time of its development.

On August 1, 1995, Awhina opened her doors. We were licensed for twenty children including five babies under two years of age. The children's ages ranged from six months to five years, and our hours of operation were from 8 am to 5 pm. We were new to the village of Havelock North. We were perceived to be different—the house was painted pink, for a start! I talked to local people who enquired as to what I was doing. "Oh, you are in the pink house," they would say. I invited a journalist from the local newspaper to visit and to write from her observations.

For the first two months I worked on my own with two, then three children. I did not advertise; I relied on word of mouth. Before long we had a waiting list, which is still the case today. We are now in a larger property, more protected and away from road noises and pollution. We continue not to advertise, and people who need to find us, do. When a visiting family asks, "Will we have a place at Awhina?" having been told of the waiting list, I reply that if they are meant to be at Awhina, then a place will become available.

Initially families came to Awhina because they saw the quality of care we and the environment offered. Today it is specifically known that we are an anthroposophical day nursery. People are warmly welcomed for who they are. There is no expectation that they have any knowledge of this education. We are simply there to provide the best for their young children—in the words of our mission statement, "to care for the child and to nurture the family."

Today I work primarily outside of the day nursery, although I still remain very much in touch with the day-to-day work with the children. (We live next door to the day nursery.) I also bring professional development to the co-workers at the day nursery, am involved with the weekly pedagogical meeting, and continue to be in the day nursery one afternoon each week as a co-worker. Without this continued practical involvement, my work would very quickly move into the realm of theory only, and the living quality that penetrates what I bring to practitioners and people wanting to embark on this worthy and very much needed task would not exist. ▣

Part 1:
A Home Away from Home

Chapter 1
What is the Anthroposophical Day Nursery?

*Nest building in mankind is as important an act as it is in the animal kingdom,
only it is more refined and much more involved.
Basically, however, it belongs to the same all embracing force,
the motherly force that pervades all nature.*

Karl König, *Eternal Childhood*, 21.

Traditionally, institutions that offer daycare to young children are called just that, "daycare" or "childcare," or "Education and Care," a new title trend that has evolved over recent years. Do any of these titles do justice to the vital task that caring for very young children implies? The naming of all things is important no matter what the initiative represents. The name is not simply a description of the institution or center, but also carries with it a symbolic picturing of the intention surrounding the initiative, a physical and a spiritual gesture.

When naming our center, the term *day nursery* brought a picture to mind of a nurturing and safe environment for little children, which would both surround and support the child's developmental path into life, as well as supporting the child's soul and spiritual development. The name *Awhina* was chosen for our day nursery for a number of reasons, the most important being its symbolism. It comes from the Maori (the indigenous culture of New Zealand) and is described in the following way. Awhina (the "wh" in Maori is pronounced as an "f") as a concept brings to mind positive ideas such as *embrace, cherish, foster, assist, benefit,* and *befriend*. The *mana* of a group or person is enhanced by the way they house, feed, and honor their guests, including strangers.[2]

---

2   *Mana* as a concept is beyond translation from the Maori language. Its meaning is multi-form and includes psychic influence, control, prestige, power, vested and acquired authority and influence, being influential or binding over others, and that quality of the person that others know he or she has. Mana may be given to whole tribes of people because they have gained a reputation for excelling in some particular area. See Rangimarie Rose Pere, *Ako*, 61.

This beautiful Maori word both reflects the gesture that is worthy of this important work and acknowledges the cultural heritage and folk soul of our country. The word is also easily pronounced and carries a soft and beautiful sound when spoken. Parents and children are encouraged to use the word *Awhina* rather than *crèche* or *daycare*.

Childcare has been part of society for many years. Childcare from an anthroposophical perspective, however, is new and is a response to the ever-changing world where family life finds itself pushed and pulled to fit society's perspective and expectations. We see little children confronted with what is seen as a normal way of life, where rushing has become the usual mode of family life. As a society we are led to believe that we have to make every moment count. There is a myth that "doing nothing" is wasting time. Children experience their parents as being in an almost constant whirl of busyness, and this is what they imitate. How is the family inspired to create a nurturing home life? Where are the positive role models?

The anthroposophical day nursery offers to the child and the family an environment that allows the child to unfold her potential in a healthy, unrushed manner, where she can learn to become truly social through empathetic guidance and supportive rhythms, and where the family can experience good, sound practices of the archetypal home. These practices can become part of their home culture if the family so chooses.

Child, Family, Day Nursery—A Threefold Relationship

There is a dynamic relationship among the child, the family, and the day nursery. This begins already at the time of enrollment before the child begins at the day nursery, when all aspects and needs pertaining to the child, the family, and the day nursery are talked about during the interview with the parents.

A biographical journey is brought to life that begins with the pregnancy and leads to the present time, listening to and understanding who this child is and where her needs may manifest. Included in the child's journey are the family's journey and situation, for these, while separate, are also one with the child's situation. We endeavor to meet the family's needs as much as possible.

By sharing the day nursery's philosophical basis, expressed in the day-to-day working, slowly a picture emerges of how the needs of the child, the family, and the day nursery can best be met without compromise of the day nursery's integrity. This relationship is continually reflected on and reviewed as the individual needs of the child and his family change, and the best solution for all concerned is sought. It is this threefold interweaving relationship of child, family, and day nursery that builds a strong and trusting foundation.

Providing childcare from an anthroposophical perspective, while primarily for the child, is also essentially about the family. It is looking to the needs of the family today, respecting their values and choices and at the same time supporting and nurturing their life of family. This we endeavor to do in a way that does not dictate, but rather provides the possibility for the parent to experience this nurturing and care through the practical day-to-day care of the child. One could say that we provide the example. We are providing a service to the parent and to the family, one that is deeply philosophically based, but which is transparent and is without any form of judgment.

Relationships

In the day nursery, much attention is given to the realm of relationships.

We endeavor to come to know the family, to begin a relationship. Through this relationship the well-being of the child is greatly enhanced. This begins with the first meeting and continues during the visiting phase, which can take as long as the parents wish—sometimes months—until the parents feel secure and ready to leave their little one, to pass their child to the caregiver who in turn becomes known to the parents. In essence, a relationship is established.

Dr. Bruce Perry writes, "As human beings we have the biological gift to form relationships" [3]—we create in the other what we are feeling. For example, the feeling of warmth that we direct to the parent is reciprocated, and a relationship begins that the child immediately experiences. We can both effect change and influence the internal physiology of the other in our empathetic responses. Today human-to-human contact occurs less and less, and the consequences of this need to be understood. Dr. Perry refers to "relational poverty" [4] as being a significant feature of life today.

In the day nursery, much time is given to our verbal communications with parents. This will vary from parent to parent depending on their circumstances and needs. What is important is that the parents know that we are there for them when needed.

When a parent steps into the day nursery for the first time, experiencing a thoroughly prepared environment, with caregivers engaged in their tasks and the children busily involved in their environment, it is these first impressions that will last.

---

3   Dr. Bruce Perry, *Brain and Mind*, 79–100.

4   Ibid.

Parents can only leave their children in a care environment when they can relate to what they see, and experience the empathy of relationship that is so much a part of the day nursery. It is the parent, on behalf of the child, who develops a foundation of trust by coming to know and experience not only the environment, but also the caregivers that are in that environment.

The relationship that is created between parent and caregiver is one of giving and receiving. The parent gives the child and the day nursery receives the child, and both must be fully and consciously engaged in this reciprocal process for the child to be able to make the transition from home to the nursery. When this transition is addressed with care and consciousness, then the child is able to take the step without discomfort or trauma. This giving and receiving between parent and caregiver takes place each day, and is based on love and trust. In the morning the parent "hands" the child into the caregiver's arms and in the afternoon the caregiver "hands" the child into the arms of the parent. It is this relationship, which in many cases encompasses the first years of life, which surrounds the child and allows a unique and strengthening sense of well-being to develop.

The Home

The child is born. Mother and father now assume a new role, that of a parent. With the coming of this child, a family is born. The house is prepared and made ready to receive this new individual. The house becomes a home through the preparation of the parents, filled with the sense of responsibility and caring that becoming a parent carries. In the past, the mother-to-be gave much time to this preparation and generally all activity surrounding this expected event was focused on the moment of the birth to come. The mother and the unborn baby were surrounded in a glow of warmth and of joyful anticipation, which included extended family, friends, and acquaintances from near and far.[5] This helped prepare the woman for the new role of motherhood, and the unborn child was bathed in this welcoming gesture of soul.

Today, baby is welcomed with joyful anticipation, but time is not always given to the soul preparation of receiving and inwardly preparing. Today's modern woman takes being pregnant very much in her stride. The mother-to-be may have continued with her work schedule up until the birth and be prepared to return to her work soon after. In many Western cultures today this is considered the norm.

The soul gesture that surrounds the newborn infant will support this little one to find her way into her new environment. The newborn's needs, certainly during the

---

5   Joan Salter, *The Incarnating Child*, 13.

first weeks, are for protection. It is the home that is the protective environment. It is during this time that mother and baby come to know one another. The relationship that began some nine months previously is now strengthened, or perhaps over these first weeks the new mother just begins to feel, to create this new relationship. This is a time for adjustment,[6] both for the infant who needs to adapt to the new conditions of the physical world and also for the mother who is adjusting to the role of nurturer, of protector, and learning what it means to become a mother. These first weeks of delicate interweaving between mother and newborn will soon pass, and the most should be made of this precious time.

We identify the home as the best environment to "cradle" the baby into life because it is one that has been specifically prepared. There is nothing that can or has replaced the home. One could call the archetypal home a *sanctuary*, a place that is holy, a place of refuge. It is all these and more.

The parents have created the space in which to nurture and raise a child, until the time is right for the little one to meet the wider world. In days gone by, the mother stayed at home with the infant for at least the first forty days.[7] Both were protected from the world and only slowly did the mother re-enter the outer world of society, and still with an intuitive protection of the infant. While mother and baby meet the world a great deal sooner these days, home is still considered the ideal environment in which to raise the young child.

Changing needs and dictates of society today, economic or otherwise, mean that the child is often no longer able to be in the home environment during these first years. If the home is considered to be the most supportive environment in which to surround the child in the most vulnerable years of life, then an environment modeled on the archetypal home—in other words, a home away from home—is the next-best environment for very young children. ▣

---

6   Joan Salter, *The Incarnating Child*, 13.

7   Ibid.

Chapter 2
The Day Nursery—
Creating a Home
for Body, Soul, and Spirit

The infant in her early months lives in the soul realm of the mother, the father, and the home. It is this realm of soul radiating from the mother that protects and enfolds with tenderness and love the vulnerable infant who is otherwise exposed to every sound, every nuance of emotion swirling around in his immediate environment. The infant is without protection and is totally dependent.

One can experience this unique motherly quality with a reverence that is only called up by the presence of something sacred. It is this mantle of soul, interwoven with the nuances of the father, which creates the environment in which the child is held. It is this atmosphere that "caresses" the child into life in the early months. Gently the mantle broadens to encapsulate the child's ever-expanding world.

When the child is brought to the day nursery, the soul mantle that mother has held around the child is folded back, so to speak, to encompass the life of the nursery with its own colors and tones, and together the family and the nursery surround the child on her awakening journey to the earthly realm, each supporting the other. This transition from home to the day nursery is given weeks and sometimes months to enable mother and child to fully embrace what is to become the family's second home.

The parent is asked to bring a biographical picture of the child, from pregnancy to the present. It is the child's life story from the moment of conception. The parents are welcome to write as much as they wish about this child. This often proves to be a very therapeutic exercise for a parent, particularly if the path thus far with the little one has been rather bumpy or difficult.

The child crosses a bridge each day, from home to the day nursery. A connection is made on a physical level—the spiritual connection is already there, for this is what has led the family to the day nursery. The bridge that the child crosses each day is a point of transition and one that needs to be prepared for in order that the child's day can begin in a calm manner, anticipating what is to come.

Just Like a Home

The first time a parent comes into the day nursery, the exclamation is often, "Oh, but it's just like a home!" One could not wish for a greater compliment. When one walks into the day nursery, one is struck by the feeling of home, and while the parent consciously experiences this feeling, the young child literally breathes it in. One also experiences a sense of harmony in the atmosphere between children and caregivers and among the co-workers. There exists a sense of beauty and attention to detail, an environment to support and enhance the child's delicate senses.

The child and parent are warmly greeted each new day, and with the caregiver, a picture is shared of how the time has been since the previous day. The well-being of the child, the evening meal, the bedtime, sleeping, and how and when the child awoke are entered into the day book (see Appendix A). How the child sleeps and how the child awakes in the morning will often be reflected in how the day will proceed. The parent will share pictures of the household that allow the needs of the child to be more fully met on that particular day, for while every day at the nursery has a quality of sameness, each day is new, depending on the well-being or otherwise of the infant or young child.

It is vital that the parent feels comfortable and relaxed (even when her own pressures cause her to feel otherwise) when she brings her child to the day nursery in the morning. The child will experience this quality of feeling in the parent along with the nuance of relationship between parent and caregiver.

From the time the child and parent step through the door in the morning, they are met with the wonderful smells of cooking, be it muesli cooking, bread baking, or fruit stewing. The food preparation has already started before the first family arrives, and to step into these wonderful aromas of cooking is a comforting way to begin the day. The mother or father leaves for the working day with a true sense of comfort, and the child steps into his day at the nursery with that same sense of comfort and well-being. The relationship between food, taste, and memory is very strong—even little children will know what day it is through the cooking smell that greets them in the morning.

The Physical Environment

The day nursery is not a purpose-built building but is, in fact, a home, having been filled with family life for many years. The children experience the day nursery in many ways as a mirror of their own home, with the different spaces used as they would be in the home for the different purposes intended. While the kitchen or dining room are used for the purpose of preparing food and meal times, they also have the possibility for play, where the children can potter about, explore, and simply be, knowing that the adult is there, engaged in the work of the home.

Stepping in

Most purpose-built childcare centers today are created on one level, allowing for easy movement from inside to the outer environment. Sadly, this gives the child little practice in his physical development in a natural way. In contrast, children and families literally have to climb up to the day nursery. There are steps leading up to the front entrance and steps leading off the back verandah—a wonderful daily opportunity for practicing movement coordination for the child...and for the parent. The possibility for natural, spontaneous movement is a must for growing children. This also asks the attending adult to be forever conscious of the child's developmental movements. Unfortunately, with more and more attention to safety issues, possibilities that encourage natural movement for young children are becoming stifled and are being replaced with contrived experiences.

The caregivers also prepare the day nursery environment with attention to the physical realm, the life or etheric realm, and also the soul and spiritual realms. It is with this preparation that the day nursery assumes the role of the archetypal home, providing a strengthening, health-giving space that allows the child to breathe in an unhurried manner, to gently unfold and find his rightful place on the earth.

Just as the home is prepared by the parent, so too is the day nursery prepared by the caregivers, acknowledging the needs of the child from a physical, emotional, and spiritual perspective. Each of these aspects needs to be nourished in a different way. Each is as important as the other. Where proper attention is given to all three,[8] then the child will develop a healthy physical body, a rich soul life, and potential to strive for a spiritual life as a free human being. As the home acts as a protection for the child, so too does the day nursery.

---

8   Veronica van Duin, *Homemaking as a Social Art*, 70.

The Culture of Homemaking

The dynamics of a home are many. The relationships that are established within the home, the archetypal picturing of the human being, the working and the playing together are just some of the vital elements that help to develop and define who we are and who we are to become. A true basis for human relationship begins in the home.[9]

When the young child's home life is shared with that of the life of the day nursery, it stands to reason that the day nursery needs to be imbued with the qualities of the home and that the nuances of the archetypal home need to interweave and surround the child. Homemaking and its task of nurturing the threefold qualities of body, soul, and spirit can ensure that this happens.

Homemaking and the Day Nursery

Homemaking is as much a part of the day nursery as it is a part of the life of the home. It is the homemaker who "carries" the home environment and who has the overview of the home, and though we are seeing a change of roles within the home environment, in most cases it is still the mother who guides and brings those qualities of nurture and culture into the home. Many fathers who find themselves in the role of primary home parent have found it helpful and necessary to develop these nurturing qualities as well. How our children are raised, the values that we surround them with, the social life of the home, will have their consequences and impact on the wider community.

Veronica van Duin refers to homemaking as an "artistic endeavor."[10] As artists we need to practice the art of creating a home, to learn about the nuances of what makes a house into a home. Everything begins in the home, and the value of the home and the place it plays in forming a healthy society still need to be acknowledged, fostered, and supported.

Childcare from an anthroposophical perspective brings with it the possibility to work creatively, to create an environment where the archetypal home is emulated and where the very young child is supported on his journey into life in a meaningful way. It provides a role model, so lacking today, for the family. It allows for homemaking ideals to be experienced, through the daily care of the child. It provides an example to be taken up in freedom. 🏠

---

9   Manfred Schmidt Brabant, *The Spiritual Tasks of the Homemaker*, 25.

10   Veronica van Duin, *Homemaking as a Social Art*, 4ff.

Chapter 3
An Overview
of the Fourfold Human Being
and Environment

Thus we have the two most significant forms of experience at the threshold of every human being's entry into the earth. The human soul enters its new house, the body, and at the portal stands a gentle guide: the milk of its mother's breast. This guide pilots the soul into the depths of the body and its functions. On the other hand, the world around the house calls for the attention of the soul. It looks through the windows of the sense organs into its surroundings. And again a guide stands ready to lead it: the human face. The human countenance opens for the baby the wonders of the world...in the human face it finds its first real hold on the world...it is from this focal point that all further impressions proceed, and experience of the world and other people is unfolded.

Karl König, *Eternal Childhood*, 67.

The Fourfold Human Being

Just as the being of the child needs to be nurtured from a bodily and soul/spiritual perspective, the life or "being" of the nursery needs to be nurtured and developed through an understanding of the fourfold nature of the human being. The human being has different aspects that make up the whole. Each of these aspects has a different task within the whole, and each needs to be healthy for the human being to be balanced and to lead a life where future potential can begin to be realized.

There is the physical aspect, that which we see. It is made up of earthly matter and chemical substance. After death it returns to the earthly substance, to the earth. Our physical body is therefore most susceptible to earthly influences. It requires constant care and attention, or illness develops. In the home environment, it is one of the main tasks of the homemaker to care for the health of the physical body.[11]

The physical body could not be sustained without something that gives it life, that holds it together, that gives it form. This principle we call the *life body* or *life realm*. Everything living has life substance around it. And so we have a physical body made of matter, engendered with a life body that gives it life. This is also referred to as the *etheric body*. While one cannot see the etheric or life body in a tangible sense as in seeing a substance, one can experience it in the newness of life in the new infant (some

---

11   Veronica van Duin, *Homemaking as a Social Art*, 26.

have described this as an "aura"). At the other end of life's continuum, in the elderly or terminally ill person, one can experience the withdrawing of life, and thus this principle can be understood by its absence. With the withdrawing of life, the physical body returns to its chemical origins, to earthly substance.

The *astral* or *soul realm* is the mediator between our inner life of feelings and emotions and what approaches us from the outside. The soul life, among other things, includes the part of the human being that creates relationships.

And then we have that which makes each and every one of us unique individuals—what is referred to as the *ego*, the *spirit body*. It is this individuality, this uniqueness that expresses itself over all else, above any physical or emotional demonstration. It is this that we meet in the other. This spirit or ego is eternal. It can be perceived as early as conception as an "essence," a dawning, that continues in its process of incarnating at different stages of life until a true birthing at around age twenty-one. It is the ego that leads the individual throughout life. It is this ego that we are called upon to acknowledge in all individuals, whatever their specific needs, thoughts, or attitudes. Without this recognition of the uniqueness of the other, of the individual, true meetings would not be able to take place.[12]

What has been expressed above in very simple terms is referred to as the *fourfold human being*.

The Fourfold Environment

The environment of the day nursery or the home can also be expressed in a fourfold manner. Just as every human being needs each of these "sheaths" to be healthy in order to complete his or her individual tasks, so do the environmental sheaths need to be developed in order for the day nursery to become a living organism rather than simply an institution. Nourishing and maintaining these sheaths is fundamental to creating a healthy whole, one which will support the child's sense of well-being as well as bring a nurturing quality that enhances the adults who work in such an environment.

---

12   Veronica van Duin, *Homemaking as a Social Art*, 25ff.

Penetrating the Environment

Creating the physical environment is the easy part of developing the day nursery. However, we need to take this a step further. The environment needs to be penetrated with a sense of purpose. All that we do, all that we provide for the children, is done with sound pedagogical reasons in mind. To fully penetrate this environment in a way that truly supports the young child, the day nursery is embraced as we would a home. Rather than seeing this work as just a job, the experience for many a co-worker is that of a *vocation*. How we choose to do this will be an individual decision. Working with a team of co-workers brings about dynamics that require a different kind of consciousness, ensuring that the myriad tasks that are required in the home environment are attended to. To penetrate the environment means to know it intimately. ⌂

Chapter 4
The Physical Sheath

The child has reached the earth...The being of the child was awake in the spirit-land;
it left that land to enter the earth, but the transition needed a threefold metamorphosis—
from spirit-consciousness through dream images to the dull period of deep sleep.
During these first months the child forgets his previous experiences.
He falls down upon the earth, so to speak, and when he gradually gains consciousness he finds himself
in a world so new and different from the previous one that the impressions it makes
upon him cover and extinguish all the tender remnants of memory of his former existence.

Karl König, *Eternal Childhood*, 50.

The physical environment of the day nursery is thoroughly penetrated and maintained in a manner that is aesthetic and filled with daily attention to detail. The little child is still very much a part of the spiritual world, in unconscious movement between the spiritual world and the earthly realm. From heavenly paradise the child enters earthly paradise. Nature is the archetypal artist, bestowing its gifts on the young child in the form of a beautiful garden. It is our human task to take hold of these gifts of the natural world and surround the child with an earthly paradise.

Rudolf Steiner once said that the child becomes what his environment is.[13] He was referring to the innate imitative qualities of the child in relation to those primary adults who surround the child. We can extend this thought further by looking at the whole environmental sheath that surrounds the child. By *environment* we mean not only the physical surroundings, but also the conditions and other influences.

The day nursery, like the archetypal home, is a reflection of the heavenly realm, awakening in the child a sense of well-being, of "coming home." Order and beauty awaken memories of the child's cosmic home in paradise, thereby supporting the child to maintain the dreamy consciousness that is so much part of the child under three years. In stepping into the day nursery, one steps into another world.

13   Rudolf Steiner, *Understanding Young Children*, 3.

The physical aspect or sheath of the day nursery is the most tangible sheath. We meet the physical environment as soon as we lay our eyes on the space. It is also what the visitor meets.

Perhaps the question needs to be asked: Have I formed a relationship to this space that has been created with the child in mind? When you form a relationship with someone you feel warmed, energized, and the same is true when you form a relationship to the environment.

How do I care for this environment? It is well known that our sense of well-being is enhanced in an aesthetically prepared work space, just as we feel chaotic when in an environment that is messy or uncared for. For the adult, walking into a prepared space should be immediately felt, immediately experienced. For children, this experience, although not conscious, contributes to their sense of well-being and can and will influence their day.

For the child, the relationship to the prepared environment brings with it a sense of being "met," of being held, of security, of being warmed—a reconnection on a different level, a connection to their spiritual origins. It is what allows the child to step into this space comfortably. Beauty is part of the early childhood years. It is important for all human beings to experience and vital for the child to be surrounded with.

When we walk into an environment that has been prepared with care, with attention to detail, we immediately feel uplifted. Sadly, it is this area of attention to detail that is more and more forgotten about today. We tend to seek for the more complicated reasons why a child may be unwell or uncomfortable, rather than looking at what surrounds the child.

Preparation

Preparation is an important component of our work, and carries two aspects. There is preparation from the outside, what we can see, and there is inner preparation, what we experience on a different level.

The outer preparation is all that is engaged in on a practical level. It includes cleaning and caring for the environment. This happens daily, in some form or other. In our homes, we prepare for visitors, because we want them to feel welcome, to feel comfortable—we want them to feel "at home." This does not just occur on its own. We need to engage our will. It might be that we bring in fresh flowers, or we may sweep the floor, or we might fluff the cushions. Whatever we do, no matter how seemingly insignificant, will make a difference. It also expresses our respect for the visitor.

In our workspace, be it the home, kindergarten, or the day nursery, the situation is no different. With respect, we prepare the space for the child in our care. In doing so, we form a relationship to the environment and we create something that is new, thus forging a deeper relationship to the child.

Inner preparation is that which we engage in in the privacy and quietness of inner contemplation. For some it is when we spend time thinking about and calling to mind pictures of the child in our care. It is often referred to as our *meditative work*, that which connects us with our spiritual origins and in particular with the child's guardian angel. The children are accompanied during their night consciousness and carried into the new day by the adult who cares for them, who cares about them.

The two levels go hand in hand and cannot be separated—the inner preparation and the outer preparation. It is this gesture of inner striving that will envelop the child. It is a gesture that is as tangible to the young child as our outer doing is for us.

And so the space is prepared. It is breathed with life; something new is created. The child is surrounded in a thought-filled manner by a carefully prepared physical environment as well as by the caregiver's inner preparation of engaging the child's guardian angel.

Cleaning

In the early days, the cleaning of the day nursery was carried out by the co-workers. This formed part of the weekly rhythm, and would be done around and with the children at the week's end. This was a bit chaotic at times, but nevertheless was a wonderful experience and one that brought the week to a close in a very worthy way.

Cleaning one's environment calls on us to look at the space differently, and therefore our relationship to this environment will change. A more intimate relationship develops, and with this our knowledge of the environment expands.

Cleaning is more than simply wanting to remove the dirt. It is about consciously trying to create something new. Removing dust and dirt results in a void, which is put at the disposal of helping spiritual beings (elemental beings)[14] who have a connection to this particular environment, in order that something new and positive may come about.[15] Cleaning as a task is such a worthy and honorable occupation when looked at creatively, but sadly, today this is seldom the case. The task is often placed in the hands of a "professional" who cleans but forms no relationship to the environment, which then does not change as a result of the cleaning. It is as it was before.

When a conscious relationship is cultivated, the space is engendered with life, which in turn enhances the human beings, the children and co-workers who live in the

---

14   Manfred Schmidt-Brabant, *The Spiritual Task of the Homemaker*, 15.

15   Linda Thomas, "Chaos in Everyday Life," 1.

space during the working week. In the day nursery we now have a support co-worker who comes weekly to help with the cleaning. She often begins in the presence of the children, who know her and sometimes help her. Her role is of equal importance to that of any co-worker, and walking into the day nursery after she has been cleaning is pure joy. It is as if the elementals are singing in unison at the attention given them. What is experienced is something new—the environment is changed, enlivened, allowing for new possibilities. It is this nuance of atmosphere that works so strongly in the life of the day nursery.

It should be stated that those early co-workers, who were engaged in the weekly cleaning as a matter of course, carried a different relationship to the care of the environment than the co-workers of today, who tend not to carry the "ownership" of the maintenance in the same way. This then has to be learned in a more conscious way. The relationship with the environment has to be created.

The daily tasks of caring for the day nursery are attended to with and alongside the children, as they would be in any home environment.[16] Attention to detail, even the smallest of details, can have its effect on the young child, and it is the relationship that we form to the environment that will enable that care, that attention to detail, to shine through, to touch the child:

> Once we learn to consciously penetrate each little corner with our fingertips, then cleaning takes on a nurturing aspect and becomes caring. And what is so wonderful about it, is that the result of caring, lasts considerably longer that the result of removing dirt! When we have taken special care of a room, the little bit of fresh dirt which is brought in, is barely disturbing, one can live with it…

> While caring for a room, we do not only come into contact with the physical world. The whole atmosphere changes, the room is filled with light. Especially children react to this transformation and they also seem to perceive the change directly.[17]

We can only enter into a relationship in a true manner if we are "awake" to what we are doing and if we are conscious that through engaging in these processes of the household we bring into play and support the work of the helpful beings of the elemental world. To understand the presence of these beings we should not enter into a materialistic picturing of what they may or may not look like. Rather, it is enough that we embrace and

---

16   Linda Thomas, "Chaos in Everyday Life," 1.

17   Ibid.

consider the possibility of something beyond that which we can see.

There are a number of books written about elemental beings that are based on human experiences, and one rather delightful story is *My Summer With The Leprechauns*, based on the true experiences of Tanis Helliwell during a summer sojourn in Dublin, Ireland.

One picture of these helpful beings that has been described is of a movement within the physical realm but beyond the physical—a stream in time of many colors. When we attend to the tasks of the etheric realm and all the processes involved in the home and of matter, it's as if this stream of color intensifies and is experienced as something tangibly felt in the very atmosphere. For many, these subtle sensitivities of feeling are, sadly, something of the past.

They can, however, be recreated and recaptured if we are prepared to take the time and the care and look beyond what is available to touch and sight only.

Children experience the elementals in a way that is totally natural to them, for it is the child who has a deep relationship to all that is in the environment, seen and unseen. When we take the time to listen we can learn so much from the child.

A Therapeutic Environment

The day nursery can be seen as a therapeutic environment, an environment for healing. We are given the possibility to create something anew each day. We begin this possibility by connecting with the world of spirit the night before, when we reflect back on the day that has been. It is very helpful if we include this looking back as part of our meditative work in the evening.

This looking back or *Rückschau* enables us to objectively reflect on the day's events, which we then take with us into the spiritual world. Our night consciousness, when entered into with an honest endeavor, can allow for a working through, a helping guide that begins to touch our daytime consciousness and brings inspiration into our life. We begin to see our environment with new eyes. We can only do this by forming a relationship to the environment in the broadest sense.

Giving the Child Space

For the child who may be at the nursery all day, the environment, both inner and outer, should offer a variety of possibilities for play and exploration as well as provide experiences that enhance sensory development. A garden filled with flowers and herbs, vegetables and fruits, which give sustenance on many levels, provides nourishment for children and adults alike. The garden preparation, planting, and maintenance are all activities that are entered into around and with the children. It is also an inexpensive way of preparing a space for little children to be and to play in.

The Garden

The garden is representative of the home garden—perhaps more how it used to be, because families of today generally manage with much smaller gardens requiring less attention, and many do not grow their own produce because of busy lifestyles. A beautiful garden is surely a child's right. To grow up surrounded by the beauty of what nature has to offer is in itself a lesson in life for little children, and for us all.

The nursery garden is full of seasonal flowers that bring delight to everyone. Summer days provide the giant sunflowers, which began as tiny seeds when the caregiver and the children planted out the sunflower pots in the spring, and which now tower above the children almost like trees. Seeds are planted in the spring and vegetables are grown. Watering and weeding are attended to daily, child and caregiver together. Fruit is harvested with the help of the children and either eaten as part of the meal or preserved for the winter months.

The cycle of the year is expressed in the garden, and together children and caregivers are engaged in the activities of looking after a garden. The roses need pruning. "We will have to get some big gloves on, won't we," exclaims a child with wheelbarrow at the ready to collect the cuttings. Yes, roses do have prickles, but this is no reason not to have them in the garden. The young child soon discovers that care needs to be taken in order not to receive a sharp surprise!

The lavender bushes, planted specifically for their therapeutic qualities, need to be pruned twice yearly and the lavender tied into bundles and hung in the sunny art room to dry. It is then stored for use in the making of soft dolls for the children. The compost heap is prepared and made during the summer months, and it lies "sleeping" until it is ready in the spring for spreading on the gardens. The growing of the "swan plant," the special plant to feed the Monarch caterpillars that transform into wonderfully beautiful butterflies, is a project the day nursery has long carried, keeping co-workers busy all summer. And so the list goes on and on and on...

The possibility to run and climb, to feel the grass beneath little feet, as well as to find quiet little corners to hide in, creates the child's world in the day nursery. This is where the child is most comfortable and happy, all the while unconsciously learning about the world, pottering in and around the garden. There are possibilities for climbing and digging, for hiding and playing, for exploring and for learning. Expensive play equipment is simply not necessary (see Appendix B).

The garden is prepared and considered in the same way as the indoor environment,

looking at the child and her physical and spiritual needs. Still only partly on the earth, the child, in her dreamy consciousness, constantly moves between the two realms of heaven and earth and therefore needs to experience something of the heavenly realm here on earth. The garden becomes a mediator between these two worlds, and therefore is a realm of beauty and grace. It invites the visitor to smell the scent of the roses and draws everyone to linger. To watch the path of a fluttering butterfly or to listen to the call of native birds are indeed sublime pastimes that are simply part of our day, shared by adults and children together. This is the garden, imbued with the call of nature that is the child's right to experience.

The garden design reflects the child's need for movement and exploration. Practicing through daily doing is part of the very nature of the child, and by doing she meets and learns to overcome all kinds of challenges. A bridge to cross, steps that ask to be climbed, a gentle slope that requires just a little slowing down if the child is not to tumble over... grass, stones, concrete and bark, sand and earth: these are all possibilities that are there for the child. Creating different spaces or garden rooms allows the children to have a wide variety of experiences in their day. Rosemary and rose geranium, just two of the herbs that are used frequently and planted on the edge of the meandering path, offer their wonderful fresh scents that the child quite naturally comes to know.

Animals in the Day Nursery

In considering animals for the day nursery, we found that the chicken family provides much that contributes to the daily lives of the children. The children with the caregiver have the experience of caring for animals—but not simply as pets, although this aspect may also develop. From a pedagogical standpoint, we want something that enables the children to come to know (through doing and example) about life in a way that is entirely appropriate to their age and consciousness. Having observed the nurturing role of the mother hen with her brood of chickens, it was felt that this was entirely right for little children.

The caring nature of the mother hen as she tucks her little ones under her wings, her protectiveness, and her giving nature were all qualities that we wanted to surround the children with. The little bantam hens are ideally suited to children. When approached, they will simply squat, allowing the children to easily gather them up. They lay well and are reasonably easy on the garden (not in the spring, however, when compost has been newly spread).

There is such joy on a child's face when the door to the nesting box is opened and there sit two or three little eggs, which are placed in the egg basket and carried carefully up to the kitchen. The joy in collecting the eggs is twofold: the discovery in the nesting box and knowing that the eggs will be used in the waffles that make Friday at the day nursery a special day.

Bantams make wonderful mothers! The anticipation while the broody hen sits on the eggs is quite tangible, and when the little yellow chicks suddenly appear from under mother hen's fluffy wings, we all breathe in the wonder that Mother Nature offers. Just as mother hen cares for her little ones, the children help care for the chicken family.

Archetypal Spaces

The day nursery, in emulating a home, needs to have the possibility of rooms and spaces that bring different qualities depending on their uses. The quality and purpose of the kitchen is quite different, for example, from that of the dining room or the place reserved for sleeping. The very atmosphere and activities that happen in a particular room enliven the space and bring with them a tangible sense of orderly well-being. Just as we often hear the phrase, "a place for everything and for everything there is a place," so it is for different spaces—for every space there is a purpose, for every purpose there is a space in which to carry out this purpose.

The suggestion is not that we follow a pedantic rule, but rather that we begin to reconnect with different spaces and how they can work on the human being in a way that contributes to our sense of well-being by bringing a purposeful doing into daily life.

Little Children Need Little Groups

Little children are better supported in small groups, and therefore several spaces are required to make this possible. Nurseries for infants away from the center of activity, a dining room, and different play spaces are all necessary, as well as a space for art and craft activities.

Each space brings with it particular qualities. The kitchen, the very heart of the home, should have room for children to be nearby safely. It is this room more that any other that invites the child in. It is a space where warmth and tantalizing aromas drift to the far reaches of the home. The activity happening in the kitchen is never contrived—it is real. Time and time again, we can see that this is the space where the child who is having difficulty transitioning can find comfort. The sitting room is the large play space, where in the winter months the rosy warmth of the fire greets the children every morning. The sofa is that comforting place where little ones curl up with the caregiver for a story or to "help" feed baby her bottle. We need to be able to offer all that the archetypal home offers.

The Orderly Task of Good Management

Order and good management are essential prerequisites in maintaining the environment with beauty and care. This should not be considered as secondary to the task of caring for children—rather it *is* the task. It is this activity filled with life and true meaning that we surround the little child with. One learns to look at the environment in a more conscious way. The co-worker looks on the day nursery not as a place of work, but as a home for which he or she is responsible through an intimate connection to the task of homemaking.

The care of the toys, ensuring that they are kept in their rightful home, mending when necessary (when appropriate, this is done with or in the presence of the child), are all aspects that directly impact the experience of the young child. We need to care about the environment, and in doing so we express that we care for the child.

Regular dusting and wiping of shelves, washing of toys, and loving care of the dollies, as well as nourishing the elemental world (which in turn enlivens the very atmosphere), all support the developing child as well as the "being" of the day nursery. Thus, we form a relationship to the environment.

Maintaining the Home, Maintaining the Day Nursery

Creating something new is not a difficult task—it is the maintaining of it that can become difficult. This difficulty arises if we allow our work to become mundane or routine. When we do something because it has to be done, without any real connection to the task, then it becomes routine. It lacks the luster of life. We have no relationship to the doing.

To be able to maintain our work and our environment, every day we need to carry love, passion, and enthusiasm for the role we have entered into. Maintaining the environment on a daily basis requires attention to detail. One example is the laundry, which is brought in from the line and then folded with the children. Hand cloths are folded one way, other cloths are folded another way, and the same applies to sheets.

It is not some pedantic whim that has brought us to this, but rather practical and pedagogical considerations. The child comes to know that different cloths are folded in different ways through observing the caregiver. Through this the child learns to differentiate unconsciously. Some cloths are used for hand washing, some may have other purposes. Some will live in the kitchen, while some have their home in the bathroom. Some are folded this way and some are folded that way, depending on where they live.

The way things are folded has been created for practical reasons having to do with how they fit on the shelf or cupboard where they live, as well as with supporting the child developmentally. This practice, along with all other practices, needs to be maintained directly for the children and their development. Working alone is relatively easy. Generally we know where we have put things and maintain an overview of process. However, when we work as a team as in the day nursery, conscious processes and organization are paramount for creating the day-to-day harmony and ordering of the environment.

Restoring Order—Tidying Away

The restoring of order after the creative chaos of play is equally important. Adequate time should always be allowed for this very worthwhile activity of tidying away. It is an activity that can often get lost in the world of busy family life. A parent will simply clean up after the child because it seems easier, or they may demand that the child cleans up by him- or herself. Both are doomed to failure in the light of educating the child.

If approached in the right way, tidying can be as enjoyable as any other part of the day. We need to enter into and embrace this time of transition with real joy and intent.

In the day nursery (and in the home), we need to carry the picture of where everything lives and live into this picture so deeply that the image will reflect in the children's souls, and they too will be moved to join with you to tidy away.

There needs to be a home, a specific place, for the child's bits and pieces. This first has to be created, so the child with the parent will come to know where this or that toy lives. Baskets and shelves are ideal for the child's room. This makes for a simple tidying-away time at the end of each day before the child goes to bed, so that what lives around the child as she begins to close her eyes is order and not clutter and chaos.

This brings me to touch on what lives in the child's room and immediate environment. Some parents are over-compensating the child today with so many toys and gadgets that the child is at a loss to even know what he has. When the child is surrounded by so much, it becomes clutter. It is far more difficult for the parent to bring about a caring attitude when there is just so much "stuff." The opposite of caring is neglect.[18] Children need to learn to care and not to neglect. For the young child, a very small number of toys, including a special doll, is more than sufficient, together with two or three beautifully illustrated books.

Little by little, these playthings can be added to over time and as the child grows. She grows into the toys she has, allowing her to form a bond and a loving relationship. When this relationship develops, the child will be more content with what she has.

A well-made toy will not break as easily as many toys do today. With poorly-made toys, children come to see that everything is expendable. When a toy breaks, it is thrown away to be replaced sometime in the future, whereas well-made, often handmade, toys can usually be repaired. The child has the experience of seeing the parent or caregiver at the nursery carefully make the necessary repairs, and just as with cleaning, the toy is renewed, given a new lease on life.

The child observes the caring gesture of the adult as the toy is made new. Now when something is broken she will expect that it can be fixed, and her care of the toy will have new meaning. One day perhaps she will attempt to repair the toy herself. Her relationship to the toy has changed, and she experiences the living gesture of the adult within this toy, albeit unconsciously.

It is the enthusiasm that we carry for the process of tidying away in the day nursery that takes hold of the children, so much so that they will want to help and become

---

18   Linda Thomas, "Chaos in Everyday Life," 2.

part of this process. How the dollies are tucked in, how the cradle is prepared, where the knitted chicken family lives on the shelf, or which logs live in which basket are all lessons of life (in miniature) that provide for the possibility of further development for the child.

There is no separation between the play of the child and the work of the child. When we omit these practicalities or do not allow the time to acknowledge where and how things are put away, then we are doing the child a disservice. We miss an opportunity to further the child's development.

How are the children to know where a particular toy lives if they are not surrounded daily with a consistency of doing, of maintaining? This allows for the child to come into the nursery in the morning and go to get his favorite plaything, because he knows, with an inner sense of security, where it will be. "Maintaining" is expressed in seeing and responding, in taking responsibility, in knowing the task, and in the element of co-working.

Finding the Balance, Bringing Support

When we truly penetrate the environment, then a careful attention to detail becomes part of our being. It is this careful attention to detail that creates a healthy physical environment. However, we need to maintain a balance.

The balance that we seek is between being pedantic and almost pathologically sterile on the one hand, and untidy, uncaring, and messy on the other hand. This does not relate only to cleaning and maintaining the environment, but to order generally. For example, are the toys placed in their rightful places, have the flowers on the table been refreshed, have the cots been made with care, has the washing been hung out with care, are the highchairs wiped down and ready for the next time they will be used?

When there exists a healthy, ordered physical sheath, the etheric or life body of the human being is enhanced. Elemental beings living in the home and garden also benefit greatly from such a cared-for physical environment. They experience a "freeing up," and become liberated, adding to the supporting quality of the etheric or life body of the human being. An already "hardened" quality in the etheric body of the human being can be redeemed and a healing can take place. ▣

Chapter 5
The Etheric Sheath

The newborn child is a stranger on earth but it is not a beginner.
The neonate is like a guest from foreign lands come to visit friends.
This guest should be received with reverence because he brings with him a vast store
of wisdom hidden under a veil of helplessness.
No tests, no rotating cameras will be able to lift the veil.
Only reverence and our humble attempts to grow near to this living miracle
will open the door to a first glimpse into the unknown world of the newborn child.

Karl König, *Eternal Childhood*, 58.

Manfred Schmidt-Brabant writes, "Rhythm is strength. And strength arises where time and life are formed rhythmically."[19] Life is rhythm and our state of well-being is governed by a rhythmical existence. Rhythm is the transition or movement from one activity to the next, from one breath to the next, from one sleep to the next, from one meal to the next, and so on. We are surrounded with rhythms that we experience in a totally unconscious way—those of breathing, of sleeping, of waking—and as long as we remain healthy, then these unconscious rhythms will remain harmonious. The etheric or life sheath of the day nursery is supported by a healthy rhythmical life.

Maintaining a rhythmical environment does not seem to be a natural part of family life for many today, and yet we need rhythm as much today as ever, especially children. In the morning when greeting the parent with "How are you?" the response, more often than not, is a breathless "Busy!" The child is immersed in this atmosphere of constant busyness.

The young child experiences a sense of comfort and security in knowing what is to happen next. Time to ponder, to find our own time into the next activity, is another precious commodity that we are all, young and old, being robbed of today.

---

19   Manfred Schmidt-Brabant, *The Spiritual Tasks of the Homemaker*, 23.

The day nursery guides the little child in a rhythmical stream that allows for a dreaming quality, which is the realm of the young child. At the same time the child is guided into a right movement through the day, which supports and ensures that the child is well rested and happy and can make a good transition back into his home environment. It is important to acknowledge that mother may be tired after her working day, and a content and well-rested child allows for a good reunion for both.

Much can be undone if, after a happy day, the home transition is fraught with tension. The parent is asked to step into the day nursery in a quiet manner, which allows for a gentle reunion to take place for the child, almost as if the parent has always been there. As the child becomes older, naturally there is a "knowing" that the parent has gone and will return at a certain time. The same transition, however, has been found to be the most supportive.

The daily rhythm at the nursery is governed by meal times. The younger the child, the more often he requires sustenance. One mealtime almost runs into the next, and being organized is vital when attending to a large group of children whose ages range from infants of around six months, to three- and four-year-olds.

The Transition from Home to Day Nursery

Transitions form a major part of a young child's life, whether in the home environment or in the day nursery. In the day nursery the transition begins with the child stepping out of the home/family environment and into what will become his or her "home away from home."

To enable the children to assimilate their new care environment, we encourage a period of visiting (called *transition visits*) before the child actually begins. These transition visits do not have to be long in duration; however, they need to occur consistently—at least two to three times during the week. What we want is for the mother and baby to form a familiar relationship to the environment, to the caregivers, and, to a lesser extent, the other children.

The parent is asked to walk through the garden, maybe to sit for a while and simply experience the nuances of this large family. As most transition visits are arranged while the children are in the garden, the parent with a baby is able to be in the indoor environment without distraction and to simply assimilate the atmosphere. She can wander freely and experience the different spaces.

As the time draws closer for her child to begin, the mother will come to know which nursery and which cot will be for her child. Little by little, the day nursery becomes a part of the family. It becomes a familiar place for the parent as well as the child. One or two weeks before the little one is due to begin the mother is given a sleeping dolly for her child, and this goes home and is placed in the child's bed.

The family is also invited to visit the day nursery garden during the weekend. This contributes to the building of a relationship, which helps to develop trust in the parent. It is this sense of trust that enfolds the child and allows for a harmonious transition into the day nursery. These transition visits may take two to three weeks or two to three months depending on the individual situation.

During these visits, the parent is asked to write the comprehensive biography of the child from pregnancy to the present. As mentioned, this is often a therapeutic activity for the parent, allowing for a reconnecting with the beginning of the child's life, and making a transition from the past to the present.

Transitions within the Day Nursery

From home to the day nursery and from the day nursery to the home are major transitions for a young child, but with the rhythm of daily doing, children soon come to experience this as their reality. Transitions throughout the day from one activity to another are carried out in a way that gently allows the child to bring each one to a completion in a healthy way: building a house, creating a puppet play, or playing with a silk cloth. When children are rushed, they become frustrated and their equilibrium soon escapes them. They will react!

By singing the children through a transition—for example, from circle-time to the morning tea table—the song becomes a familiar link from this activity to that, and because it is used daily, it helps to bring one activity to a close and begin another in a manner suitable to the being of the little child. This kind of transition, which occurs without the child even being aware of it, is the type of rhythm that speaks to the child.

Being guided through well-balanced breathing-out activities, such as the playful movements of a stamping circle game, and in-breathing activities, such as a quiet story on the sofa or a puppet-play beside the fire, contributes to a harmony of being in the young child.

The sleeping dolly mentioned above plays a key role in the link between home and the day nursery for each child attending more or less full-time. The dolly goes home with the child each day to be placed in his or her cot or bed and returns each new day to accompany the child into the day nursery.

Sleep–The Mediator

The rhythms of the day nursery are determined somewhat by the ages of the children, with the infant under twelve months normally having two naps in the day, while the toddler over twelve months is able to play and potter through the morning until near the middle of the day. This can be very individual.

Preparing the little one for sleep is entered into with the utmost care and the undivided attention of the caregiver. The singing of a much-loved lullaby accompanies this time. Baby is wrapped and carried to his nursery. Through experience we feel that the modern child needs the extra protection that wrapping affords, and it has been our experience that the baby and toddler comes not only to expect this enfolding, but in fact longs for it. The baby-wrap acts as another layer of skin for the modern child whose own body sheaths are often not healthy.

The child is carried to the nursery in the horizontal position—a picture of what is to come. The curtains are pulled, with the caregiver quietly saying "good night" to the garden, to the chickens, to the sandpit, all those realities that exist for the child. A gap is left in the drawn curtains, allowing for the light of day to enter and for baby to experience his surroundings upon waking.

The Nurseries

Baby is placed in his crib where his sleeping dolly is waiting, and is tucked in with a woolen quilt and blanket in the winter and a light woolen blanket or cotton sheet in the summer. Each baby has his own cot that remains in the same place in the nursery. Each cot is surrounded with a folding stand, a sheath of protection placed around the child. To ensure that the baby has his own physical and "breathing" space, the cots are placed in the nursery in a way that respects the child's sleeping environment. As a rule, the nursery has only three or occasionally four cots. Again, this depends on the needs of the individual babies in that particular nursery. The room has been warmed prior to sleep time, and a small window is always left slightly open to ensure the freshness of air in the nursery. A hot water bottle may be used to warm the cot prior to baby going to bed.

Sleeping babies are (visually) checked at least every ten minutes. When we know a baby is unwell, we check more frequently, including physical checks as needed. The child's caregiver comes to have an intimate knowledge of the unique needs and how illness manifests in the individual child, and will attend to those needs accordingly. (See Appendix C for remedies stocked in the Awhina Healing Basket.) Sleep monitoring is recorded in the individual baby file (for babies under twelve months) or the day book, showing times of checking and length of sleep, as well as how the child slept.

Sleeping for the Older Children

For the older children (those no longer in their own cribs), the large playroom is transformed into a prepared sleeping space while the children are in the garden and sometimes with some little helpers. The play toys and equipment are carefully placed aside in an orderly fashion to allow room for sleeping "houses" to be created. This is an area enfolded with a protective folding stand, which the child sees as his or her sleeping space.

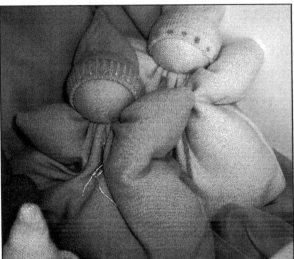

Attention is given to the making of the individual beds, which each has its own sheet, blanket, and woolen mattress cover. Beds are made in an aesthetically pleasing way that invites the child in, and the child's sleeping dolly is waiting there. Chest rubs are administered when needed. The child is tucked in and supported to sleep—the adult singing a lullaby and guiding the child to an independence in going to sleep, slowly withdrawing but still consciously present. The caregiver will remain in close proximity to the sleep room, conscious of this space at all times. The carrying ego of the caregiver surrounds the child and allows for a warm security to enfold the child.

Sleep and the Modern Child

Sleep is something of an issue for many modern children. They have difficulties in finding sleep, are restless and fidgety and require time to unwind, time to reach a point of being able to rest. Repeatedly we see children intently engaged in play that includes "going to sleep." How carefully they prepare their sleeping space and the amount of layers they place over their bed in preparation never seems to be quite enough for what they need. Is this a symbolic gesture by the child, asking for more protection on a soul level?

These children are supported to go to sleep with massage or simply stroking, using therapeutic Weleda oils. Massaging of the temple is very soothing for some children, while for others it is the busy feet that will only come to a point of rest when gently massaged. There are those children who do not like to be touched, and for these children an "etheric" massage is given—the hand moves in slow, long strokes two or three inches above the body. Alternatively, the caregiver sits beside the child, gently holding and stroking a dolly, particularly the sides of the temples. When this is carried out with a thorough consciousness, the child will soon fall asleep.

The sleep room indeed becomes a therapeutic space, prepared for children whose lives are busy and in many ways overextended. In the day nursery it is a common experience that on Mondays, after weekends spent sometimes almost constantly on the go, the children are overtired and fragile.

Awaking–A Precious Time

The transition from morning to afternoon, with rest or sleep being the mediator, allows for a completely different type of play to happen in the afternoon. When the child is quietly content and well rested, the play has a quality of centeredness. Sleep has wonderful restorative qualities, especially for the child in the care environment, where being social is part and parcel of each day. This is yet another argument for having the possibility of different spaces and enough adults in the environment.

The transition from sleep to waking is very important for the sense of well-being in the young child. How a particular child awakens needs to be respected—some are awake in a flash and are ready to be in the world, while others (and experience shows that more and more children fall into this category) are not ready to awaken, do not wish to awaken, and would prefer to stay in the safe world of sleep, wrapped in their woolen blankets.

These children need to be gently guided to awaken and allowed to take their time in finding their way into the world. Upon awakening, the child is "bathed" awake with Weleda lotions or oils (depending on the season), supporting the child in the movement from sleeping to waking. Following the hygiene rhythm of diapering or toileting, the child is dressed, and hair is gently brushed. Again experience has shown that more and more children are extremely sensitive in the head realm, and great care needs to be taken when brushing or combing the hair. With the consistency and strengthening of these awakening rituals, the child is now ready to be with the other children.

The rhythms of sleep vary according to the age of the child and need to accommodate each individual. To fully support the child, no matter what age, one has to know the individual needs and respond as necessary.

A Daily Rhythm

The day's rhythm is akin to breathing, and generally begins indoors where the little child feels secure and can reconnect with the environment. For the child who arrives at 8 am, it will be the stirring of the bread dough that has been resting over night and now needs to be prepared for baking, or the folding of the washing, which the child may have helped hang out the afternoon before. On a Monday morning, the little ones like to follow the caregiver who prepares the cots, all time chatting comfortably and "knowing" the environment—knowing whose cot is being made, knowing the routine, for this is their home...their home while away from home.

At 9 am it is apple time, and the children, seeing the fruit bowl handed to a caregiver, immediately come and surround her. The ritual of the "doing" is something the child connects with and in fact needs as guiding and strengthening points through his day. Together they sit, adult and child, sharing pieces of apple, sometimes chatting but mostly quiet, intent on what they are doing.

The morning play time continues around the caregivers, who may assist the children when necessary but who usually are engaged in the life of the day nursery; this may be preparing the morning tea, or mending a broken toy or dolly. It may be putting an infant to bed, or perhaps folding the washing or doing the ironing—in other words, all those activities associated with the archetypal home. These are activities that "build" the day nursery, bringing life into the space, life-filled doing that strengthens the growing child.

Simple songs and rhymes that the children love to sing and move to are brought in the course of the morning, sometimes independently in smaller groups and sometimes together. Rhythmical games of movement bring the child into language in a natural and supportive way—for example, "Ring Around the Rosie" is much loved by little children who love to "fall down" as a cosmic memory of their incarnating process.

The puppet plays again are simple, repetitive stories that even the smallest children come to know. These plays are brought to the children at the same time each year and are closely associated with the seasonal and festival calendar.

Hygiene Rhythms

Little children are still gaining control over their bodies and the hygiene rhythms of pottying and diapering. These, as well as hand washing, are very important considerations in their day. The child is introduced to good hygiene practices at an age when it simply becomes part of what happens naturally. The caregiver supports the child in good practices, and when the child is ready and able, the practices and foundations laid will allow the child to be responsible for her own hygiene in a healthy way.

It seems to be the trend today for little children to be able to do things for themselves at a very early age. Children are expected to be independent earlier and earlier, when in fact they are at an age where they still need the guiding hand of an empathetic adult, helping them to find their way, guiding them to become competent in what they do. True independent competence can only arise in the child who experiences the nurturing helping hand of the adult during these early years.

In the day nursery it is the adult who with care and attention washes the child's hands. The child feels the nurturing care that a conscious adult brings. This giving by the adult, this attention to detail such as washing carefully in between little fingers, warms the child who little by little will take steps to become independently able when the time is right. The gesture of the adult surrounds the child with well-being and a growing self-esteem.

Those transitions where care needs to be taken to support the child in a healthy way, such as the movement from diapering to potty to toileting, are guided in an organic and relaxed manner through "listening" to the child. This listening mirrors the child's awakening consciousness to this step in development.

In the day nursery the child is not "trained" when it comes to the potty or toileting. When it is noted that the child is having dry diapers from one change to another at around two to two-and-a-half years, then the child is invited to sit on the potty (or toilet). This is offered in the form of a statement, which is carried as an intention by the adult and guides the child to follow through. The child hears the clear statement coming from the adult: "It's time to sit on the potty." We guide the child with our inner intention, rather than offering a choice. This becomes a rhythm that the child happily sees as part of the diaper change procedure.

On the other hand, if the child feels any form of pressure—perhaps the parent is anxious to shift the process forward—it is our experience that the child will decline and the process will inevitably take much longer. There needs to be a continuing and open dialogue with the parent, who may feel anxious and who will value the reassurance given by the caregiver. When the parent is anxious, the child too will sense this and become anxious.

The same applies to the cleaning of teeth. It is the adult who guides the child in the right use of the toothbrush, and the child can contribute in other ways such as holding the brush for the toothpaste and drying the tooth mug after it has been rinsed.

Rhythm and Food

The children, even very little ones, come to know which day it is by what is being cooked. Bread is baked almost every day, the dough rising overnight. Different grains are served, having been prepared the day before and soaked overnight. The child is supported with the optimum nutrition gained from Demeter (see Appendix D) grains and produce, including seasonal vegetables from the day nursery garden.

The meal seldom changes, with slight seasonal variations only. For many children, the food served is not something they are used to or in some instances have even tasted before. However, experience has proven that in time and with patience on the part of the caregiver, the child comes to eagerly anticipate the food prepared with love and with a consciousness of its growth and life forces.

Meal Times, Nourishing, Sharing

Meal times are pivotal times of the day. They are social times of sharing, a daily festival. The table is prepared with care and beauty and is a feast for the eye, indeed for all the senses. It is these times that the children connect with and love the most. It is an activity of the senses, and it is often this aspect of the day that the children will first relate back to the parents when asked about their day. One could describe the coming together and sharing of the meal as an activity that provides nourishment to the body, soul, and spirit.

Children and caregivers all sit together to share this time of being social and of eating together. Babies who are awake join us at the table as well. Babies, still in arms, are not usually brought to the table, which at times can be just a little too "social" for them. Those babies and toddlers who are ready and able are seated in their own special highchairs, acknowledging the journeying aspect of the incarnating little one. The highchair carries almost a sacred quality that gives a profound and deep respect to this little one. When the child is older and more fully "on the earth," he will then come down from the highchair and sit on a chair at the table, where over a period of time his feet grow to touch the ground.

For children in care situations, it is important that the rituals of home life such as sitting down together to share a meal are emulated. It is important that the food preparation is done with and around the children, allowing the child to experience this. The giving of time and attention to what happens in the kitchen is in danger of being lost in many homes today. The preparing of food is an etheric process that has an artistic quality.[20] When given the possibility of being part of the preparing of the food, a conscious activity by the adult, the child has the potential to develop a different relationship to food and its preparation in the future.

Morning teatime begins with the lighting of the candle. This simple ritual helps create a mood, and speaks to the children that something is going to happen. The adults and children quietly join hands together (those that are ready and able) and the *karakia* (a blessing in Maori) is sung.

This simple but meaningful practice allows a moment in time where inwardly we, the adults, acknowledge the food we eat, in gratitude for its goodness and how it has been grown. This is not something we bring to the children; however, this becomes an unconscious inner experience for the child.

Children love the ritual that a song or a gesture brings. It is this moment of pausing that can change what might have been a noisy transition to the table into a quiet group of little ones eager to begin their morning tea.

After eating, the table is cleared in the same directed and careful way, observing those children who want to help, always being mindful of the "how" in our doing, aware that we, the adults, are also being observed. The child will immediately follow and imitate us. Do we want the child to carry one cup on top of another, two cups in one hand, or do we want the child to carry one cup in her hand?

Sharing food is one of the most important aspects in life for most people. It nourishes us, but also has the added advantage of bringing us together around the dining table as a family—an opportunity is created for social interaction. It is this same social dynamic that is sought for the children in the day nursery. Meals are prepared together with and around the children. Adults and children sit down together at the dining table.

There is a clear distinction made in the planning and preparing of meals for children under and over twelve months of age. When an infant comes to the day nursery (around the age of six months), the parents provide milk or baby formula (if possible of organic origin). When baby is still breastfeeding, mother will bring her expressed milk in bottles, or she may choose to come into the day nursery to breastfeed. This will depend on her work situation along with the needs of her infant.

---

20   Manfred Schmidt-Brabant, *The Spiritual Tasks of the Homemaker*, 18.

Any solid food that baby is having is brought from home for the first two to three weeks, before a transition is made to food prepared at the day nursery.

Meals for the youngest children may consist of lightly stewed fruit (morning or afternoon) along with mashed or pureed vegetables. Carrots[21] can be used exclusively for the first year if no other organic vegetables are available. A wide range of vegetables may be given from around five months of age. The combination of vegetables for any given meal is determined by the need to have a representative from all three groups: root, leaf, and fruit/flower.[22] When choosing fruit for the baby, we check that it is tree-ripened, is grown in season, and that it has been grown to ensure the maximum life forces. Around their first birthday, the children will start partaking in the meals prepared for everyone at the day nursery.

It is not our practice to include meat or fish in our menus[23] in the day nursery because of the high protein and fat content, which for young children is more difficult to digest. We do include eggs in the waffle mixture served on Fridays for morning tea, using eggs produced by the day nursery's own hens. The menu includes various grains, a wide selection of vegetables, and nuts and nut butters (avoiding peanuts),[24] which are all fine sources of protein for growing children.

The children are served water and herb teas made from herbs such as lemon balm, peppermint, and pineapple sage, which are just some of the herbs that can be grown very easily. Apple peel tea is also a favorite of the children. These teas are always served warm to support the child's warmth organism, which at this age is not strongly developed.

Potatoes, a member of the nightshade family and a swollen stem rather than a true root vegetable, are not recommended for children due to their taxing effects on the brain.[25] A variety of grains and sometimes sweet potato (known as *kumera* in New Zealand) are good replacements.

---

21   Petra Kühne, *Säuglingsernährung*, 41.

22   Rudolf Steiner, *Nutrition and Health*, 4.

23   Kühne, ibid., 71.

24   Ibid., 65.

25   Ibid., 72.

In the day nursery honey is used very sparingly for little children. It has a loosening effect right down into the digestive system.[26] Dried fruit, homemade jam with reduced sugar, and nut butters are used instead of honey. Generally, sources for protein, carbohydrates, fats, and minerals can be found in a variety of foods (see Appendix E).

Reuniting Parent and Child

As mentioned previously, the parent is asked to re-enter the day nursery at the end of the day with a quiet respect rather than in an excited manner. While the parent may be excited to see the child, through experience we have come to see that a quiet reunion is supportive not only for the child but also for the parent. This is being respectful of the environment created specifically for the child, as well as respecting the child and the sense of well-being gained from the environment. For some children the moment of reunion can be quite emotional, and it is for this reason that the parent is asked to step into the day nursery in a way that allows the child to have an experience as if the parent has never left.

Rhythm brings a comforting sense of security to the child. In cultivating consistent, breathing rhythms we also strengthen the etheric sheath of the day nursery, home, or kindergarten. However, in all this we need to be mindful of a creating a balance.

Finding the Balance, Bringing Support

In the rhythmical sheath the balance is sought between repetition without any aspect of renewal on the one hand (we could call this *routine*, where we simply are doing for the sake of doing because "we have always done it like this"), and chaos on the other hand, where next to nothing is the norm, a "go with it and see what happens" approach. When the day nursery is enlivened with a healthy rhythmical sheath (this includes biodynamic management of the garden), then the soul life of the co-worker is experienced as being enlivened. Out of a sense of chaos there rises a feeling of satisfaction. ⌂

---

26 Petra Kühne, *Säuglingsernährung*, 28.

Chapter 6
The Soul
or Astral Sheath

During its first year the infant's consciousness is utterly different from what it will be later on. There is as yet no ego or self-consciousness. There is no here or there, no "I" or "you," because everything is a united whole. It is a general consciousness that is sometimes like a light, sometimes like an image, one moment dreaming then again sleeping, swaying to and fro.
Perhaps a color appears, a finger, a pain, hunger or light, a human face...but nothing remotely akin to "I" or "You" because everything is one. And only when the child, anxious to sit and later to walk, has attempted its first steps, only then do world and body gradually begin to separate. However this separation is still not yet into "I" or "You" or into "mine" or "thine," but one object is here, another there, yet both are still "mine."

Karl König, *Eternal Childhood*, 102.

The soul of the day nursery is the realm that embraces the social, sharing, and co-working aspect. It involves creating a warm and welcoming environment for families as well as co-workers. It is about relationships—human to human, as well as human being to environment and environment to human being. It is the soul sheath that enables the person to know the environment, to feel comfortable, to feel at home. This is as true for the co-worker as it is for the parent. In the day nursery setting, in the home, or in the kindergarten, it is in working together that we support the child—a simple statement but not always so simple to achieve. Working together in harmony requires a certain consciousness, a certain wakefulness and awareness—first of all, of oneself.

Knowing the Environment

In the day nursery we aspire to create a home for the child, a space imbued with all the qualities that make such an environment more than simply a house. It could be called an "organism," a prepared space that includes the physical realm, the etheric being, the astral element, and the spiritual entity.

A well-managed household brings a sense of comfort and security. This usually comes about not by good luck, but by a conscious endeavor, which requires a contribution in some way from every member of the household. This, in turn, allows for a tangible atmosphere of warmth to permeate the home, while chaos and disorder will produce an atmosphere just as tangible but not so pleasant. The day nursery environment, too, needs to be penetrated with consciousness for the right atmosphere to be created.

So what is this realm in which I find myself working? What is an anthroposophical work environment? Such an environment is one that has been prepared with love and with empathy for the child as well as the co-worker. The preparing of such an environment could be compared to that of the family who prepares for the coming of the new baby and all that this entails. It is with this much attention that we prepare.

Coming into such an environment for the new co-worker or new practitioner has been described by some as "stepping into" a place that feels familiar, that has a quality of welcome. It is a place where love and trust are integral. This way of being may be new for people who have not experienced a work environment where the quality of humanness comes first. Therefore they will need to learn to trust, and this can take time. It is only with love and trust that the adult can truly walk alongside the child, supporting the child on his or her incarnating journey.

Co-working

In my home environment I am required to work with others. It may be a roommate, or it may be a husband or partner as well as children. In order to live and exist cooperatively and harmoniously, through our love for the other, there is give and take; we learn to make compromises. When the taking is out of balance, disharmony arises.

In the work environment, while we each have our own tasks, there will be times when we overlap with others. A co-working environment can be a place where our "comfort zone" is shaken. We need to become aware of the signposts along the way that require us to become awake, to look at ourselves, at who we are and at how our actions may impinge on the other. Do I see myself as "co-working" or do I see myself and my task as something that has nothing to do with anyone else?

When our comfort zone becomes a little unsteady, we are being given a gift, an opportunity for meeting and for working on our own development. It is not that these opportunities don't happen in other work environments, but the conditions that are present may not allow for them to be truly taken hold of. We are free to accept this gift or not. In entering an anthroposophical work environment, we are also being given the opportunity to walk a path of self-development. And this opportunity is even greater because of the need to work together with others.

Co-working means looking at oneself honestly. It also means looking at the other and sometimes seeing oneself. In co-working we learn to acknowledge our strengths and weaknesses. It means becoming active participants in developing answers to the challenges that face us, rather than ignoring or turning away from them. Taking hold of these challenges gives us the opportunity for personal growth.

If our working together is truly founded in Anthroposophy, we cannot choose to ignore the situation or the person. If we do, the result is that one or the other person feels forced to leave and the pattern of behavior is again repeated in the next work situation. There is a transparency that cannot be avoided when working in a way that acknowledges the whole human being from a bodily, soul, and spiritual perspective.

Thoughts and Feelings

Our feeling of discomfort when a difficulty arises permeates the whole environment, and in some way will affect other co-workers as well as the children in our care. We need to assume responsibility for our actions. We need to also assume responsibility for our thoughts, which could be described as "unactioned deeds," and which cannot be hidden from children. Children connect strongly with what our thoughts hold. They are not fully on the earth but still on the path to the physical realm from their spiritual origin. To believe that we can hide our thoughts and feelings is a falsehood.

The child will warm to a loving, thought-filled approach by the adult, just as the child will immediately sense when the thoughts or feelings of the adult are tinged with an inner emotional struggle or, worse still, antipathy. We fool ourselves and do the child a disservice if we believe we can cover such thoughts with a contrived smile. Young children have a perception or clairvoyance that is beyond the grasp of the adult.

We live with and work with the need to create a balance and a harmony of being that allows for our human qualities to shine. We can achieve this by being healthy in all aspects of our own threefold humanness, in order to live and work harmoniously with the other, our fellow co-worker. Bringing balance into our life is a key to maintaining health. When we are too much in the spiritual realm, too lofty, then we dream our way through life. We cannot grasp the realities of the world. We cease to be practical. We need to aspire to greatness (or at least goodness) in our work, but in doing so we also need to have our feet on the ground.

On the other hand, when we are too much in the physical, our thinking becomes materialistic, and we see only what is before us and not the wider picture. We cease to see the person's ego, the striving behind what we see before us. We tend to meet situations for what we see rather than what can be.

In an environment where people are required to work together, it is the soul realm where the balance can so easily be tipped. This is the realm of relationships. It is this realm of the emotions where the elements of antipathy and sympathy are at work. We must take hold of this realm if we are going to be able to work with others.

Working in an emotional way, in the realm of judgment, has no place in our work with children. It is entirely inappropriate to allow antipathy or sympathy to enter into our relationship with or around the child. The same naturally applies to the adult. An unhealthy relationship develops out of either polarity.

With excess sympathy we draw the adult or child to us out of a personal need to feel good, to boost our self-esteem. This also makes for a difficult relationship between the child and other co-workers. By being antipathetic, we turn the adult or child away from us and we cut off the possibility of a true meeting. Sometimes we turn away unconsciously because we cannot cope with what this situation brings to us or how it makes us feel.

The following poem, "That Other Self," expresses this beautifully:[27]

Behind you, behind me
Stands you, stands me.
Sometimes for a moment I
See the self behind you.
Do you too ever see
The other self behind me?
Time holds his breath,
The chatter fades.
False seeming,
Self esteeming,
Fear and the pose that we adopt
Or hide behind:
The veil is dropped.

---

27   Dorothy H. Lillico, *Perspectives*, 16.

Then for a passing moment I
See the self behind you.
I wonder, do you ever see
The other self behind me?

In the interpersonal realm where one is working intimately with others, the life of the soul and all the emotions that come with it can so easily come to the surface, particularly when one is stressed or tired. Rather than deal with the emotion, we turn away. It may be through a lack of confidence, or fear of what we may meet.

Inner Work of the Adult

When we experience a difficulty with someone we work with or a child we cannot connect to, it can be most helpful to picture this person or child prior to going to sleep. Additionally, looking for a positive quality that may have been overlooked allows for a new way of working the next day. This is our inner or meditative work.

Some people use certain verses or exercises as tools to support their daily work. A short verse or invocation can be most effective, such as, "I will strive to do better tomorrow." In this simple deed one can, during sleep, connect with the spiritual world and receive the guidance to strengthen one's resolve to work with the difficulty. What is important is that we believe that what we are doing will make a difference.

One of these tools is called the "eightfold path"[28] (see Appendix F), where each day has a particular quality that one strives to raise consciously into the will. These exercises can quite easily be incorporated into the day (first thing in the morning is a preferred time) and can become real inspirations for supporting our journey through the working day. *The Calendar of the Soul*[29] by Rudolf Steiner is another such tool for meditative working.

Co-working means giving and taking. It implies trust, and it means supporting the other as you yourself would want to be supported. It is not about being better than someone else at doing this or that. It is about knowing yourself, about knowing your skills and your weaknesses and being able to admit to needing help or support. It is about being open to receiving the other's gifts—which may be a helping hand, a

---

28   Rudolf Steiner, *Knowledge of the Higher Worlds*, p. 137ff.

29   The *Calendar of the Soul* consists of fifty-two meditations following the soul's experience of the year. Several translations are available.

suggestion, or a cup of tea—or it may be, on a deeper level, about being able to share your gifts with others.

In the day nursery, as in the home environment, our work is completely transparent—we find ourselves in situations that require action or response, and we are called on to act in the moment. Being different in personality, in temperament, in age, we each will have our own way of responding. Gender also needs to be acknowledged; much research could be done on the qualities that the male brings to this work realm and likewise the qualities the female can offer. We have fundamental differences, which, when explored, can only support our co-working as well as offer a possibility for addressing the present imbalance of male/female in this profession.

We learn not to make judgments about others. Judging tips the soul balance and teaches us nothing, and we move nowhere. When we find ourselves in such situations, often we tend to point to what the other did not do or contribute to the situation, rather than ask the question, "Was what I did helpful or could I have done this differently?"

I only have the possibility to change something in me. I cannot change the other person. Good co-working is supported by a work environment built on trust, by knowing the work environment and by knowing the task. It is this orchestration of conscious, living activity that will support the child as well as the adult in the environment.

The Community of the Day Nursery

Working with the infant and very young child is multifaceted and is like the weaving of an invisible fabric, with each warp and weft thread vital for the coming together of a fine garment with which to clothe those in our care. When one of the threads breaks or is forgotten, then a hole will appear. We might not see this at the time, but it is there and in some way it will manifest. Co-working is akin to a community weaving—if one element is missing in the community (of the day nursery or the home), then a gap will occur.

On the surface, the element of co-working looks simple; however, what appears simple and straightforward to the visitor often requires the most work. The ingredients that are needed to transform the physical environment are easily brought together, just as maintaining a good, sound rhythmical sheath is not so difficult. It is the invisible element of co-working within the astral or soul sheath that requires the most effort. When this element is strong, it imbues the environment with the qualities needed to surround the young child.

The Emotional Needs of the Little Child

Creating the right out-of-home environment for infants and young children presupposes that we know what their needs are. The physical needs are transparent. We can ensure that the child is warmly clothed when necessary, and that nutritional needs are met with care to the preparation of the food, and that the produce used is of the best quality. The environment is one that is safe, while allowing for the little one to explore. Being safe does not mean being without challenges! Sadly, the child's world is being turned into a regulated environment where rules and regulations assume a greater and greater focus. This takes away the freedom of the child to make mistakes, to fall over and pick himself up, which is necessary in the process of finding his way. The child learns to place himself in the world by meeting and overcoming challenges.

Physical development is dependent on the child being able to engage in these challenges, to practice, to overcome, and then to move forward, all the time guided by empathetic adults who measure the challenge out of an intimate understanding of the child, allowing the child to move forward on her journey, at her own pace. The outer world of the child is attended to in all that we meet in the physical environment.

Meanwhile, the child's inner world, the realm of soul and of emotional development, needs our utmost care and attention today, particularly that of the very young child whose vulnerability and well-being is totally dependent on the caregiver. Who we are and what we represent to the child will have a direct influence on who that child becomes.

It is not true that our thoughts and feelings dissipate, leaving no impression on the environment—it is our thoughts and feelings that in a sense develop the nuance of the environment. This can be experienced when we walk into a space created with certain activities in mind. Take for example a church and its atmosphere of peace, quiet, and sanctuary: one immediately is enveloped in something that is quite tangible to the soul. On the other hand, imagine a motel room, a space where people come and go continuously with little purpose except to sleep. One experiences the four walls, almost a sense of isolation, and not a lot more. The human quality is lacking. Each environment, each space has its own "feel" or atmosphere, and each affects our soul life accordingly.

One has only to walk into the room of the new mother and baby to experience a soul atmosphere that is acutely tangible. This could almost be expressed as a "sacred" moment—one's voice softens and the footstep lightens. It is as if one is in the realm of the angels, the very atmosphere surrounding and enfolding the infant, much like an invisible but very tangible mantle. Within this mantle are warming, weaving colors, radiant and light-filled. For the young child this mantle is a spiritual reality.[30] It enfolds and deeply affects him.

The mantle (or atmosphere) that a mother surrounds the infant with is no imaginary picture, but a reality. The infant experiences himself as part of the mother,[31] sharing her soul life fully during the next months and to a lesser extent over the next two to three years. If mother's soul life is calm and joyous, so too will the little child be affected. If mother is nervous and anxious, this will also express itself in the child. It is an intimate relationship, with each subtle change of mood bringing a different nuance of color.

---

30   Joan Salter, *The Incarnating Child*, 91.

31   Ibid.

Father participates too, interweaving his own particular colors and tones with that of the mother. This mutual sharing of soul forces, sometimes surging and stormy, at other times calm and peaceful, creates the soul environment in which the child is enfolded.

For the child in the day nursery, the environment and the primary caregivers carry this mantle of soul warmth, providing a quality of security and protection—not replacing the mother, but rather walking alongside the mother, sharing in caring for this little one. This requires that the caregiver maintain equanimity in her attendance and care of the child. In the day nursery we call this "working with warm objectivity." This way of working requires ongoing personal development, which is a fundamental requirement for the caregiver working in the anthroposophical day nursery.

Relationships, Attachment, and Primary Caregiving

The first three years of the child's life are of crucial importance. Children need stable emotional attachments with primary caregivers, as well as spontaneous interactions with peers. When these experiences are lacking, development, both of caring behavior and cognitive capacity, is damaged in a lasting fashion.

The modern world is different for children today. While modern technology has provided opportunities for children in various ways, the negative impacts of this technology, such as the endemic use of the mobile phone, are causing a decline in extended family life, family meals, and spontaneous peer interactions. This is depriving many children of experiences that promote positive growth of the cognitive and caring potentials of their developing brains.

The growth of child care, now seen as a normal way of life for more and more children, demands that we be serious in our endeavor to ensure that the child, particularly in the first three years, is surrounded with key (primary) relationships that will allow him to grow into an emotionally healthy individual.

In an article in the journal *Brain and Mind*, Dr. Perry stated that there are three key capabilities that must be present for our species to survive: individual survival, procreation, and protection and nurturing of dependents. The primary strategy we use to meet these objectives is to create relationships. It is through these interdependent relationships—with our families, communities and societies—that we survive and thrive. In other words, we need each other. Human beings need other human beings!

Perry describes the first three years as a time of great opportunity and also great vulnerability for expressing the genetic—and, I add, spiritual—potential in the young child. The brain develops in a sequential and hierarchical fashion; this means that each brain area will have its own timetable for development. The implications for this are profound.

For the development of socio-emotional functioning, early-life nurturing is absolutely critical. If this is absent in the first three years and the child is subsequently adopted and begins to receive attention, love, and nurturing, these positive experiences may not be enough to overcome the mal-organizations of the neural systems mediating socio-functioning, Dr. Perry states. What happens in the home and the role of the homemaker (whoever fulfills this position in the life of the family) will thus ultimately have an effect on society.

What Is "Attachment"?

There is a special form of emotional bond that we call "attachment." The way we attach to others determines the quality of our relationships and how we view the world.

Our attachment styles and patterns are grounded in our first experiences, those primary relationships of our first years of life.

Attachment is the essential bonding of the baby to the key people in her life. It is not a style of parenting—it belongs to all babies. This first relationship is usually with the mother, but it can in fact be with anyone. Attachment is reciprocal; the mother receives it from the infant and the infant receives it from the mother.

There is much information about the types of attachment relationships, and it is important for early childhood educators to have an understanding of secure and insecure attachment styles. A healthy attachment relationship forms when there exists:

Proximity: Being available when needed; this implies a fully conscious "being there" and not simply a physical proximity.

Sensitivity: "Attunement," learning to correctly sense unspoken questions; this asks that we be attentive in our observation.

Responsiveness: The relationship blossoms and expands as we respond to the needs of the child and when we carry a warm interest for the child's family.

Attention to the "primary relationship" within the day nursery needs to be our priority.

The Primary Relationship within the Day Nursery

The role of the primary caregiver for the very little child, within the supportive circle of co-workers, enables the children in our care to be individually and collectively "held" in our daily consciousness. Primary care does not mean exclusive care; it means that all parties know who has primary responsibility for each child. Just as in a family, we all together surround the child with the mantle of loving care.

We need to be aware of all types of children. The busy, noisy child "asks" for our attention, but what about the quiet child, the so-called "good" child or the child who does not ask for relationship? It is these children who can so easily be missed who also need a consistency of care, touch, and loving attention. This requires that we be awake to what the child is asking of us, and that we give him not what he wants but what he needs.

Let's use the example of the clingy child who wants to be picked up constantly. The child may be unwell, or teething, or there may be difficulties in the home situation. The child has good reason to be clingy. However, if the child is well and is picked up all the time whenever he makes the slightest noise, he will demand this attention. This is not working with warm objectivity; rather this is working with an over-sympathy that does not support the child or the child's relationship with others. How the child is responded to at home is an important consideration here.

The primary caregiver needs to be awake to such behaviors through the intimate working with and relationship to the child and the understanding of what is meant by warm objectivity. Only then will we come to know when the child *wants* to be picked up and when he *needs* to be picked up. Through a consistency of response the child comes to trust in himself and in the world. He becomes independent at his own pace—not too early, which can lead to later emotional difficulties.

The "primary" relationship we have worked with at Awhina has specifically been for the little one up to and around the age of eighteen months, depending on the child. Our co-working model has allowed for the children to connect with other co-workers if they so choose after this time.

We consciously maintain this primary relationship for the duration of the time that the child is at the day nursery. This ensures that no child slips through, particularly the "good child." The co-working model as we have developed it at Awhina means that each practitioner is "carrying" four or five "primary" children.

The primary caregiver has the task of leading the "full" child study (for the full-time child in the day nursery) as well as smaller studies recording daily happenings in the life of the child, including observations and significant photos. These are contributed to by all practitioners, who keep reflections and observations in their files. We need to remember that while written observations are a wonderful resource, our primary concern is the child and not the paper!

Homemaking as Relationship-Building

Homemaking can be defined as an activity that allows us to form a relationship to the environment and to the other people who either work in or come into the environment.

From time to time it is good to reflect on the relationship you have to your own home. Does it excite you, warm you, or depress you? Which space in the home do you feel most connected to? In which rooms does the joy of family life come to the fore? Which space do you dislike to go into?

In forming a relationship to the space in which I live or work, I need to "lend" myself, to care for the space and attend to it in much the same way that I do with human relationships. I also need to know what the space is used for and warm the space with its rightful use. When we show interest and take care of the environment, we develop a relationship to it, and the child experiences this as an enlivened sense of belonging and of "being at home" in body, soul and spirit.

As Dr. Bruce Perry says: "Healthy attachment capacity is not enough to create healthy socio-emotional functioning. Attachment is only one form of the many relationships we form to create a healthy productive life." [32] The environment itself has an effect on our emotional and physical life and our sense of well-being. It is this relationship capacity that we want to surround the growing child with. Relationship is all-embracing!

Preparing for the Child

Just as the mother's inward preparation during pregnancy is important, preparation on a soul level that "speaks" to the new little one, so is the preparation of the day nursery important if we are to be ready for the little child who enters the nursery. The infant's origins lie in the world of spirit. This past existence remains the greater part of

---

32   Dr. Bruce Perry, "Childhood Experience and the Expression of Genetic Potential," 95.

the very young child as he slowly awakens to his earthly home. During these early years the greatest care is given to one so very vulnerable to environmental influences. In the day nursery, the sanctity of the child's spiritual entity, as much as the physical and soul realm, is acknowledged with the greatest respect.

The gradual movement from home to nursery, which sometimes begins with the mother in pregnancy, allows for the mother and child to experience the atmosphere of the day nursery that has consciously been prepared. In no way does the day nursery endeavor to replace what only the parents can offer the infant. However, what we can do is add to what is already part of the child's world, and in doing so enhance the life of child and his family.

Developmental Steps

It is during the third year that the child develops what Rudolf Steiner refers to as "the feeling of 'I'."[33] The child begins to sense her own separateness and begins to play with the word "I." We can envisage this cover of soul warmth folding back as the child continues her steps in independence, little by little, stepping out into the world and recognizing her own identity. With imagination, one can almost see the modern child pushing back this mantle herself in an eagerness to step out into the world. A new chapter has begun. The heavenly forces in which she had been so fully immersed now relate to her in a different way.

We see changes also on the physical plane with the growing maturity of the brain.[34] It is the day-to-day experiences of babies, infants, and toddlers that orchestrate the development of their brains, and emotional well-being and brain development go hand in hand. The play of the child becomes more creative and more and more involves other children. Little by little he explores the environment. Infants raised in a safe, nurturing environment will be stimulated by these experiences, which in turn spark brain cells into action and wire the crucial connections between them. These experiences then become translated into permanent changes in the structure of the child's brain.

Our understanding of brain development, and with it the child's emotional needs, should be our prime concern if we are to truly assume a responsible approach to the care of infants and young children. Simple experiences such as talking, singing, and reading to children, as well as encouraging and reaffirming their emerging skills,

---

33   John B. Thomson, *Natural Childhood*, 220.

34   Joan Salter, *The Incarnating Child*, 92.

caressing, cuddling, and playing with them are just some of the ingredients required for healthy brain development, the power of which can be seen in babies and infants who shine with an eager curiosity and delight in life.[35]

Caregiver/Child Ratio

The emotional needs of the young child are fulfilled by the caregivers' responses. This implies that in the day nursery there will be sufficient caregivers to be able to give a response!

The infant who cries and is uncomfortable due to teething, the little child who falls and needs comforting, each learn to trust that the caregiver is always there and always available. The day nursery philosophy has always been that the little child in need, regardless of what that need may be, should only have to turn to see a beloved caregiver.

It is for this reason also that substitute caregivers are not used, unless they are known to the children. The day nursery ratio is ordinarily more than is required by the Ministry of Education of New Zealand, and when there is an absence, a healthy co-working team is able to "tighten up" their working and fill the space left by the absent co-worker.

The aspect of co-working plays an intrinsic role in this realm and is pivotal to the healthy life of the day nursery. The giving and taking, the acknowledging of the other, are key qualities in fulfilling the role of co-worker. The economics of child/adult ratios must *never* override the emotional needs of the child.

Knowing that the adult is always there allows for the children to live into the care environment with trust and security, and this in turn allows the children to simply be, to fulfill the task that is theirs at this stage of their life, that of finding and connecting with their earthly home.

In heaven shines a golden star,
an angel led me from afar
from heaven high, unto the earth
and brought me to my place of birth.

These are the words of the song that we sing to the children on their own festival day, their birthday. The child comes to the earth from realms of the spirit...*in heaven shines a golden star*...a symbolic gesture of the journey of incarnation, from the heavenly

---

35   Dr Robin Fancourt, *Brainy Babies*, 13.

realm to the earthly realm, to the home of mother and father, parents already chosen by the child—a connection made in the heavens.[36]

Today the parents look to the day nursery to help care for the child as well as to support them in their task of parenting. The work of the day nursery is as much about nurturing the family as it is about caring for the child. From the moment of stepping through the gate we walk a path together. Together we care for the child. Together we support the child's journey into this earthly life, sometimes expressed as the child's "incarnating journey."

Finding the Balance, Bringing Support

Strengthening our social skills and relationships in order that we may connect with others in a meaningful way allows for a co-working that is free of all judgment. It is this quality of humanness that supports the astral or soul life of the initiative, in this case the day nursery.

A healthy balance is sought between a hierarchical structure and a "false democracy"—between simply being told what to do on the one hand and a lack of leadership on the other. When the soul life of the initiative is healthy then so is the co-workers' sense of spiritual well-being—a sense of disorientation becomes a feeling of "being at home." 🔲

---

36   Karl König, *Eternal Childhood*, 17.

Chapter 7
The Ego Sheath

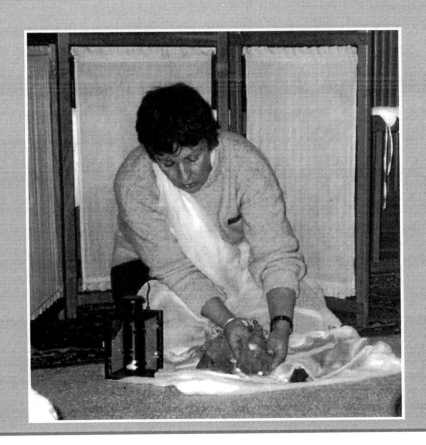

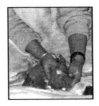

We have now become aware that to be a child can only be characterized
by that existence of Man which undergoes perpetual change, which constantly metamorphoses.
However, it can only be realized if those who occupy themselves practically with children do so
in an ever-renewed spirit of true devotion.
Thus the forces of childhood have to spring forth from within, to grow, to flower
in ever new metamorphosis, thereby forming something which is complete in itself.
This is the first thing which, however, can only happen if enough love, enough sympathy
from the surrounding is developed towards the child.

Karl König, *Eternal Childhood*, 100.

Philosophical Basis

The day nursery has a spiritual element that we will call the "individuality" or ego. For the day nursery to remain healthy, the sense of ego, of individuality, needs to permeate all areas. The ego of the day nursery—its motif, aims, and purposes—needs to be transparent to all who wish to work in this environment. It is the individual co-worker and her understanding of the philosophical foundation that strengthens and nourishes the ego of the day nursery.

In the day nursery, where people come to work for many and varied reasons and not necessarily because they have a connection to the philosophical foundation, it was noted almost immediately that if the aims and aspirations of this initiative were to be upheld and maintained, then professional development needed to be offered on a continuing basis. This is entered into on a daily basis through mentoring and role modeling, and on a weekly basis as part of the pedagogical meeting.

When professional development, including mentoring and role modeling, are not happening regularly, then the principles and practices of working with young children from a threefold perspective very quickly become diluted.

It is important that co-workers are aware of the spiritual intention and the ego foundation from the very beginning. While one is not expected to become a practicing anthroposophist (although this may well happen in due course), what is non-negotiable is this foundation. The practices may need to change, but the inspiration for the ego foundation does not. The co-worker who is placed in the leader position and who carries the responsibility for training of other co-workers needs to have a strong relationship to the philosophy, in order not to undermine the spiritual intent of the day nursery community.

Our place in the world is also part of the picture. Each country has its particular history and its own particular landscape that interweave to create its own unique character or culture, its own personality or folk soul. At Awhina, *Te Whare Tapa Wha*—the Four Cornerstones of Health from the Maori perspective—are acknowledged with this in mind (see Chapter 8).

The Pedagogical Meeting

The weekly pedagogical meeting forms the heart of the day nursery. While it is an opportunity for all co-workers to formally be together, it is expected that all (full-time) co-workers will attend. We reflect on the week passed and the week to come, study together, look at particular children, and share openly and honestly our working relationships, reflecting on both positive and difficult issues. The meeting begins with a verse by Rudolf Steiner:

> *The healthy social life is found*
> *when in the mirror of each human soul*
> *the whole community finds its reflection,*
> *and when in the community*
> *the virtue of each one is living.*[37]

We call on the spiritual world to assist in our human deliberations, strengthening our inter-working, for us as individuals and for the children in our care.

Creating an environment of trust, expressing a warmth of soul, supports the ego (individuality) of the co-worker and thus enables the co-worker to embrace the being of the child with a worthy and supportive gesture. Many early childhood practitioners know from personal experience how taxing life with little children can be. Working with a group of people is very supportive for the individual, who learns to share responsibility rather than assume it alone.

---

37   Rudolf Steiner, *Verses and Meditations*.

The regular pedagogical meeting is one of the most important vehicles of communication and is vital to connect the day-to-day happenings of the day nursery, as well as becoming that sacred vessel into which a "Christ-like" working can permeate. Sitting around the table together, reflecting, sharing, and questioning, can be a highlight of the week that brings inspiration for the new week to come.

When we work in an anthroposophical environment we are in a Christ-centered realm of objective love, which carries respect and an acknowledgment that each person is intrinsically good and well-meaning. It may also bring the courage to question or confront the other, when necessary.

Equality and Guidance

We are all equal as human beings, equal in the respect and dignity due to each individual. While we have equality as human beings, this equality may not extend to our professional capacities. Some of us may be better prepared for certain tasks, by virtue of experience, training, or study. We therefore need to allow for these people to lead and to guide. There could be a number of skilled people who are each able to lead and guide, each in his or her own particular area. We need to be able to recognize and acknowledge each other on this basis, in an atmosphere of love and trust.

Training and study are entered into on the basis of enabling us to fulfill our task in a professional manner. This should always allow for something more to be "entered into," enabling a response that does not become egocentric or elitist. The work with infants and very young children in an out-of-home care environment is a profession, and as such needs to be prepared for and supported by training worthy of its ideals.

Self-care

The area of self-care is very important, and can also be seen from a fourfold perspective. We have the responsibility to be fit and healthy for our task, in all layers of our humanness. This requires good nutrition, adequate sleep, and home rhythms compatible to work rhythms. Each co-worker is responsible for her own self-care.

If our soul life and relationships are maintained in a way that allows us to step into the new day in a rested and peaceful mode, this allows us to leave any residual personal concerns or conflict at the gate. These personal issues simply do not belong in the nursery. We also need to be responsible for our personal and professional development and our life of study. This involves our relationship to and understanding of the work environment.

The inner path of meditative/spiritual development is entered into in personal freedom and cannot be part of a job description. For those actively engaged in a meditative realm, there is no doubt that this way of working gives support and allows a truer connection to the needs of the children in our care. Through this we also develop a greater understanding and empathy for others. Engaging in contemplative study, which may begin with just ten minutes a day, provides support for the soul life and brings strength to the ego through creating a possibility of renewal in the spiritual realm.

Self-care is also about balance, balance in our life of work and balance in our times of not working. We need to ensure that we are fulfilling our work tasks, while at the same time not overworking to the point that our personal or home life is put at risk. We could say that it is about being a good manager of our time. The problem is not that we do not have enough time. The problem lies in how we manage the time we have.

Is there a component to your work where you get to experience your fellow co-workers socially? This allows for a coming together in a different way that often brings with it a new understanding of the other, which can bring a warming support to the co-working relationship.

What makes me feel good, uplifts me, and brings enthusiasm into my life? For some it may be going to a concert, for others going for a walk along the beach, or it may be allowing yourself time to engage in a loved activity like painting. Whatever works personally for you needs to be included as part of your daily or weekly plan as a matter of course, and not only to "patch things up" when you are nearly at the end of your tether.

The area of self-care should be held with as much importance as any other area. An unhappy or tired co-worker reflects on everyone including the children. Other possibilities to support self-care are included in Appendix G.

Finding the Balance, Bringing Support

In the ego realm, there needs to be a balanced and clear picturing of the philosophical foundation. When the identity of the day nursery and what it represents is transparent and understandable, this strengthens the ego of the initiative. A balance is sought between fanaticism or dogma, where there is no room for change or development, and an attitude of carelessness, with no clear vision and organization.

Childcare from an anthroposophical perspective may arise out of an independent initiative or may be affiliated with or sponsored by an already established school. Either way, there needs to be a sense of independence where the day nursery can develop its own culture built on the needs of the family, the work of the homemaker in relation to the home, and the needs of infants and very young children. Each co-worker needs to be open to this way of working and actively continue his or her path of personal and professional development so that the philosophical basis of this work is supported and strengthened.

This completes the picture of the fourfold aspect of the life of the day nursery: the physical environment, and all aspects of the spaces, both inner and outer; the etheric realm, as revealed in the various activities and the rhythmical life within and around the nursery; the astral realm of the soul, tangible in the quality of relationships, in the aura of the household; and the spiritual realm, in which a feeling for the task, and the philosophy strengthens the very foundation of the day nursery. When all four environmental sheaths are developed and maintained, bringing a sense of harmony, then the spiritual being of the day nursery can fully incarnate. ▣

Part 2:
Principles and Practices at Awhina

Chapter 8
Principles of Good Management

*To put it in an image we could say that every childhood or youth is like a garden which begins
to sprout, become green and later on to flower. This process continues uninterruptedly
from the time when winter ends to deep into the summer. The world and all the stimuli
that come from Man are like the sun, moon and stars looking down on this garden.
Light and warmth, frost and cold, wind and rain, thunder and lightning,
all flow into the developing plant and only when the blossoms appear, when colors emerge,
is the plant completed. Childhood and youth are then finished
and to become adult is nothing but the answering maturing and fruiting of everything
that has grown and developed since childhood.*

Karl König, *Eternal Childhood*, 101.

When one is working with a group of people (co-workers), what is important
for the harmonious management of the day nursery is that all have a clear
picture of *what, how,* and *why*. While the practices described in this section
may appear to be very detailed, it has been proven over and over again that when
working with a group of at least five people without a clear written picturing of the
task, practices begin to fall away and attention to detail wanes.

The *what, how,* and *why* need to be penetrated down to the smallest detail in order
to support not only the children in our care but also the co-workers, and ultimately the
day nursery. These details may be as small as how one puts away the garden tools or the
dustpan and broom. When these have been returned to their rightful home, then the
co-worker does not waste precious time looking for where they might be. There are a
myriad of such small tasks in the environment of the day nursery.

With good management, stressful situations are alleviated, the day can progress
smoothly, and this brings a sense of "knowing" and satisfaction that, although not
always consciously acknowledged, will become conscious when something is not in its
rightful home. We awaken to our own needs, and in doing so awaken to the needs of
our fellow co-workers.

These practices and procedures need to remain living, and this living quality
is maintained through regular reflection and review. Without a living process of
maintaining or renewal, the practice will fall into the realm of routine and will cease to
serve the living entity of the day nursery.

What follows are some areas of practice and procedures that have been developed for the day nursery over many years out of an anthroposophical understanding of the needs of the little child. They are offered here as guiding tools only. They are reviewed annually and more often when necessary, and these practices guide co-workers in all that lives in the day nursery. This review process, while an expectation by the Ministry of Education in New Zealand, also ensures a "living" working. When one is working with living sheaths as expressed in the fourfold motif, then when an area of the day nursery is unhealthy, one determines quickly where this lies and where attention is needed.

These practices are quite comprehensive, because they have been refined and penetrated continually over a period of time. If you are at the beginning of this work, you could simply take elements from what follows and with personal experience build up slowly over time to create your own practice.

Philosophy, Purposes, and Aims

In New Zealand every childcare center is required to have a written statement of philosophy. This is usually just a few lines, but because of the "special character" of Awhina I have chosen to give a full description of who we are and what we represent. Even if not required by the state, it is worthwhile to create a written statement of the philosophy behind what one does on a daily basis. The following can serve as a model and inspiration for others who are searching for the right words to describe their philosophical background. The fundamental principles of anthroposophically-based childcare are described in more detail in Chapter 16.

The Awhina philosophy is based on the indications of Rudolf Steiner (1861–1925), the Austrian philosopher, scientist, and educator. His spiritual-scientific research is known as *Anthroposophy*. This, simply stated, means, "wisdom of man." According to Rudolf Steiner, the human being is a threefold being of body, soul, and spirit, whose capacities unfold in three developmental stages on the path to adulthood: early childhood, middle childhood, and adolescence.

Education from a Steiner (Waldorf) perspective began in the kindergarten for children of four years and older. It is only over the last twelve years or so that the need for care of the very young child in an out-of-home environment has been acknowledged and developed, Awhina being the first such center in New Zealand.

At Awhina we are providing an environment as close to an archetypal home as possible. We approach our work with the young child very much in the mode of the mother, where the child experiences the attitude of empathetic caring vital for healthy emotional development. While we carry the motif of the mother, we work with warm objectivity that requires a conscious balance between the soul qualities of sympathy and antipathy. Homemaking and the role of the homemaker, with all that this embraces, are pivotal in our daily work with and around the children in our care.

Small children, unprotected, are at the mercy of their immediate environment. Their whole body acts as a single sensory organ,[38] unconsciously uniting external impressions with the internal world of the child. The child's body also acts as a sensory organ for the individual—the soul and spiritual being. The interaction of external impressions with the child's internal organ development is revealed in the wonderful power of imitation with which every healthy child is born. Every perception is first deeply assimilated, then grasped with the will and reflected back to the outside in echo-like activity.

As caring role models and practitioners we need to be concerned with two important considerations. The first concern lies with the protection of young children and the sense impessions that surround them. The second consideration is that of guiding the child gently into life by allowing the child to learn from life and for life—hence the importance of surrounding the child with caregivers worthy of imitation.[39]

In the Awhina environment, young children are given the opportunity to develop at their own pace and learn through imitation of the adults surrounding and caring for them. Good role models encourage impulses in children through their very gestures,[40] through their very doing. Children model their behavior on the examples they see around them.

---

38 Rudolf Steiner, *The Education of the Child*, 18.

39 Ibid., 22.

40 Edmond Schoorel, *The First Seven Years*, 214.

Overview of General Practices

What follows here is a distillation of the practices that were arrived at through the experience of the actual "doing" from day to day in the day nursery. Several of these topics are further explored in Chapters 9 to 14. For thoroughly penetrating our practice, "pedagogical papers" or "working papers" on various topics proved a useful tool. These were brought to the pedagogical meeting for discussion and reflection. For more on this process, including an example of a pedagogical paper and a response by a co-worker, see Chapter 15. Every center's description will be different and will arise out of particular circumstances. Again, the practices developed at Awhina are offered as an example.

The *family grouping* concept allows mixed ages of children to work and play in smaller groups and in different spaces. In this way children have the opportunity to learn social interactions with peers as well as older and younger children. We believe that it is more supportive for young children to be in smaller than larger groups of children. Therefore we have created the possibility for a number of play spaces where the children can play and interact in their own way and at their own pace according to their ages. The majority of children may (but not always) come together only at circle time or for a puppet play, at meal times, and in the garden.

Rhythm is integral to our philosophy and essential in the care and support of the young child. The daily rhythms of meals, play, toilet, rest, and so on, as well as procedures connected to care activities such as diaper changing and sleep rhythms, are expanded upon on a weekly, seasonal, and ultimately yearly cycle. A breathing rhythm provides the child with a sense of belonging, a sense of security, as well as sense of time and space. This in turn allows the child to venture out and to interact with the environment in a meaningful way that warmly supports the child's development now and in the future.

Singing and movement support the child on her developing journey. During the morning, children and caregivers may come together in song and in movement. The song of the human voice[41] touches the child's soul in a way that recorded music does not. This is a time for well-loved nursery rhymes, seasonal songs and verses, circle games, gesture games, and puppet plays. Speech and language development arise in the earliest stages out of the child's movement[42], the gestures of the adult, and an environment where the child experiences clear, accurate, and rich language between adults on the one hand and children on the other.

Nutrition is important on more than a physical level. Meal times are social times. Food is prepared with and around the children, with love and with care. This in turn supports healthy eating habits, as well as healthy digestion and organ development. We use produce that has been grown biodynamically or organically, when available. The early years of growth and development in the young child are so vitally important in that they lay the foundation for the child's future, and we believe that only the best available is suitable.

The garden and immediate environment are cared for and maintained by the co-workers with and around the children. The biodynamic preparations are applied to the garden and compost throughout the year. The garden provides the young child with a host of opportunities for learning, development, and support of the senses. It provides challenges for young children in their physical development. It provides a wealth of sense impressions, delighting the sense of smell—the child's first meeting with the outer environment. The garden also provides some of our daily foods such as herbs and vegetables, oranges, mandarins and lemons, feijoas, apricots, and figs, as well as quinces

41   Joan Salter, *The Incarnating Child*, 78.

42   Rudolf Steiner, *Understanding Young Children*, 8.

and crab apples for jelly-making. The chicken family is integral to our garden. Their care and maintenance, the daily collecting of the eggs, and the rearing of the chickens each spring are just part of the rich outdoor experience created for the children. The caring for the environment allows the children to experience a holistic nurturing, a sense of *Mana Atua* (in Maori, "acknowledging the spiritual") that permeates and surrounds all that happens with and for the children in our care.

Children not only learn by participating in these everyday activities and experiences, but they also begin to include and re-enact these in their everyday *play*. In play, children develop skills and their faculties ripen. Here the powers of initiative and creativity, which are important for the whole of life, are nurtured at their very source.

In the realm of *health*, a mother-and-child nurse is available to parents in an advisory support role. First aid for minor bumps and scrapes are treated with Weleda medicaments. Staff members update their first aid certificates as required.

Resources for parents include workshops on various topics such as soft doll making, parenting, "creative living with the two-year-old," and the festival table. Awhina Cottage Craft is our little shop, promoting organic knitted clothing for infants and little children, including slippers and woolen vests. We have a range of soft dolls for different ages and other playthings suitable for little children. Awhina newsletters are brought to parents bi-monthly. They are filled with the happenings of Awhina and serve as an important means of communication to parents and community.

Professional development for staff at the day nursery is an ongoing process. This may take the form of anthroposophical study, child development study, the planning cycle, the festival year, seminars, and artistic activities including speech, handwork, painting, and eurythmy. The pedagogical meeting takes place weekly. This meeting oversees the life of Awhina in all aspects—for example festivals, the rhythmical life of Awhina, children and child studies, daily and weekly reflection, and administration. All co-workers are expected to be part of this meeting.

Festivals, including seasonal festivals, the Christian festivals of Easter, Whitsun, Advent, and Christmas, as well as the child's own festival, the birthday, are acknowledged at Awhina and celebrated in a way appropriate to the child's developing consciousness.

The unique *culture* at Awhina breathes life into the environment prepared with the young child in mind. This culture is imbued with an anthroposophical picturing of the human being, acknowledging the threefold aspect of body, soul and spirit. The culture that is Awhina acknowledges all who come in their individuality and their uniqueness. Culture for the young child begins with the home and family and is broadened through friends and neighbors in the community. The children and families who come to the day nursery become part of our culture, and Awhina forms part of the culture that surrounds the child and family. A right attitude and love and respect for every human being who crosses our path will allow for the child the same attitude and love and respect.

As part of our culture, we cultivate *Te Whare Tapa Wha*, the Four Cornerstones of Health from the Maori perspective. This represents a conscious effort to embrace the bi-cultural heritage of our country Aotearoa (New Zealand). It is the spiritual motif from the Maori perspective, the four elements being the motif of the family, the physical realm, the soul realm and the spiritual realm. From these cornerstones of health arise those elements of life that live strongly in the Maori and in every human being.

In these live the following:

Mihi: the stepping through the gate for the young child is like a spiritual memory, a transition from the past to the future, the connection to Mother Earth.

Karakia: a prayer acknowledging our coming together, sung as a ritual before morning tea.

Whakapuaki: through story we greet and also embrace the child. These simple stories from life we call *incarnating stories*.

Whakarata: we assume the guiding light for the child with our sense of ego. We guide and support the child into life.

Whakaora: we come to know the child intimately, and through this we nurture and guide. Our care of the child encompasses that which the parent has shared with us—the child's biography.

Whakaoti: reconnecting on a spiritual and physical level.

Whakatangi: to safeguard and protect.[43]

At Awhina, we are on a journey, a cultural journey in time that will continue to evolve, a journey that will allow the interweaving of spirit to find its rightful place. ▣

---

43   Awhitia Ropiha, "The Four Cornerstones of Health as Related to Awhina."

Chapter 9
The Role
of the Co-Worker

At Awhina we aspire to create the qualities inherent in the archetypal home. Our work is in the mode of the mother and our task is that of the homemaker in a home environment. In the day nursery we have an intimate way of working, where respect for the human being is paramount for the child, the family, our fellow co-workers, and the environment. The caregiver does not replace or interfere with the parent/child relationship, but rather contributes to and supports it with a warm objectivity. In our working we carry the image of respect and consideration for the families who come to us as well as our fellow co-workers. Awhina is there for the family as well as for the child.

The co-worker should at all times bear in mind the Awhina philosophy and the picture of the human being as a threefold being of body, soul, and spirit, as given by Rudolf Steiner. All that we do for, with, and around the infants and young children in our care is done carrying this picture. Fundamental to this is the understanding that the young child's mode of learning comes about primarily through imitation. The co-worker is therefore a role model for the children at Awhina, and needs to consciously carry this important aspect of the work, which includes all that he or she does, from the very gestures that are used to inner attitudes and thoughts.

All that is done in the course of the day at Awhina, whether it be preparing the food, baking the bread, gardening, or cleaning, needs to be imbued with a joy, enthusiasm, and empathy that not only includes but also embraces the children.

Daily Tasks of the Co-worker

The co-worker's daily tasks at Awhina may include the following:

- Cooking, baking, and the preparing of meals with an awareness of the nutritional needs of the young child from a general and an anthroposophical perspective

- Having a knowledge of the different plants in our garden and an openness to organic and biodynamic methods, including composting

- Preparing the kowhai (arts and crafts) room by providing suitable activities for young children, in relation to the time of year, the festival celebration, and the age of the child

- Preparing circle time in relation to the seasonal and festival time of the year, with the emphasis on movement, seasonal songs, and nursery rhymes, as well as the gesture games by Wilma Ellersiek

- Preparation of puppet plays, including making and maintaining puppets and having an understanding of the plays for young children

- Tending to the hygienic rhythms and needs of infants and young children, e.g., diaper changing, toileting, the careful washing of hands, cleaning of teeth, and so on

- Knowledge of and openness to the use of Weleda medicaments, both those used daily in the day nursery—arnica, hypercal, combudoron cream and gel, plantago/eucalyptus chest rub and catarrh cream, diaper rash cream, and calendula cream—and others used not so frequently

- Administration, including the maintaining of certain records such as toileting/diaper charts, sleeping checks, attendance register, accident book, immunization register, and the day book

- Administration and care of both parent and co-worker libraries—this may include reviewing books from time to time for the parent newsletter

- Maintaining personal information and planning files as well as contributing to the center planning file

- Being familiar with and having a working knowledge of *Te Whaariki*, the early childhood curriculum

- ▲ Maintaining confidentiality at all times, with regard to the children, families, and co-workers, as well as daily issues surrounding Awhina

- ▲ Having an awareness of the emergency procedures (posted on the parent notice board), including the Earthquake file (in the staff resource file)

- ▲ Participating in the co-worker appraisal/reflection process—a two-way approach to maintaining a healthy working relationship among co-workers on the one hand and between co-workers and management on the other

  Aim: to assess and improve, where necessary, the professional status of the co-worker

  How: by sharing our practices and our questions at weekly pedagogical meetings, with openness and with trust

  Outcome: to create and maintain a healthy environment of work

Planning for the Very Young Child in a Group Situation

What does *planning* really mean? Do I know my role? Do I know where I should be at any given time? Being aware of our tasks should become second nature to us. At the same time, our tasks should not become fixed; rather, we need to become aware of the needs of the children and respond accordingly. We need to make our tasks rhythmical, while at the same time maintaining flexibility. These tasks need to be carried out bearing in mind the needs of the child, the needs of the group as a whole, as well as those of our fellow co-workers. We consistently carry the microcosm/macrocosm picture—our task and its value at that particular time, and the needs of the whole. Each co-worker is but part of the whole, and each co-worker contributes to the environment that is the day nursery.

The Awhina day is a series of movements in transition. In order for the transitions to flow smoothly, considering we are working with little children, we need to know our place, know what the need is, and carry an overview of the whole in order to see the needs of the few. Little children are guided in these transitions by the adult. When the adult is unsure, then the child becomes unsure. An unsure child is an insecure child who shows this insecurity through some degree of discomfort—through crying, in a very little child, or unruly or inappropriate behavior in the older child. Often at these times of transition we let go of the child in our conscious holding. The child experiences this letting go immediately, and it is this that creates inharmonious transitions.

Here are two examples. Baby Emily is having difficulty finding sleep. She is in a different sleeping nursery than usual—has this been prepared consciously? Baby Margot's rhythm has changed. Has her up-to-date day rhythm been noted? Is there a conscious awareness that this will affect her going-to-bed time?

Group and Individual Planning

Planning is twofold. On the one hand, there is planning as part of a team. I need to know where I am going to be. Will it be in the playroom; in the dining room working with salt dough, ironing, or cutting up fruit; or in the kowhai room, engaged in painting or perhaps in handwork preparation for a birthday? Generally we move to or fill a space that needs filling. There are key co-workers who tend to be in certain places, and the child becomes familiar with this. Co-workers acknowledge this, and after checking, one may place oneself where the need arises.

For example, there is a group of children in the dining room and no co-worker, or there are three co-workers in the playroom. What should be the response? We need to see the situation and respond. Is the play chaotic or creative? This can be reflected in the noise level, but not always. Sometimes the noise level may be quite high and the surrounding play very creative. We need to look at the whole and respond to the needs as they arise.

This, in essence, is co-working. I look at the needs of the whole and place myself in this picture. We must lose any element of egotism, while at the same time holding on to our sense of ego, our sense of self, which is experienced by the child as a guiding, caring mantle.

On the other hand, there is individual planning. Taking into account the planning cycle and associated considerations such as *Te Whaariki*, the Early Childhood Curriculum for New Zealand, and "Desirable Objectives and Practices" (both these documents are regulation requirements), I make my personal plan. I ask the question: "How can I care for this home environment in a way that ultimately supports the children?" Questions for my individual planning process might be:

▲   Do the feeders need mending?

▲   Have the dollies been checked and maintained?

▲   Are the trucks/trains being maintained, are there hooks or other parts missing?

▲   Do the play clothes need attending to?

- ▲ Will I make a puppet play which involves puppets, cloths, and their preparation and perhaps some collections from nature?

- ▲ Are some new additions for the dolls' house needed?

- ▲ Do we need to make more twisted newspaper for kindling?

Let us take the last example. One could plan for this activity by thinking about:

- ▲ Which space is appropriate for this activity?

- ▲ Where will I find a basket for the rolled kindling?

- ▲ Do I need to gather the newspaper?

- ▲ When will I do this with the children and for how long?

- ▲ To ensure that hands are washed following this activity, will I prepare a basin with warm soapy water or will I take the children to the bathroom?

Goals for Planning

Individual plans are brought to the pedagogical meeting to share and for possible input from co-workers, as is the review after the event. Our planning and reflection process, as well as ensuring our preparedness for the child in our care, provides for a transparency of working. It can also become a valued resource in the future. Both plan and review are kept in the co-worker's file.

Our planning needs to be simple, and it will naturally have some similarity to the care and maintenance of the home. It is this planned picturing that you are able to engage in when a moment arises that allows the space and time, the first priority being the children. With practice, we learn to do both. We need to be aware that we do not become so engaged in our activity that we forget the children. We also need to be able to drop what we are doing if we need to respond to a situation.

Our planning should involve an element of the season of the year. We need to plan both for the inner space and garden environment. It is not necessary that the children do activities with you; however, your consciousness needs to embrace the children and allow for some entering into your work by providing pieces of wool, fleece, card, and so on. All materials can be contained and tidied into a basket at the end of the morning or when you need to finish.

Your planned intention or activity may cover a period of two to three weeks or longer. It is the consistency of the activity, the conscious doing, and the follow-through that works on the child in such a positive way.

Whatever planning we decide on, we need to invite the child into our activity. In fact, this should always be our gesture, in all that we do, whether it be folding the blankets or putting away the mattresses after sleeptime: we take the opportunity to invite the child. This is done not by verbal entreaty, but by way of gesture.

Our task should not be seen as a means to an end—it is the activity we must live into. The child cannot differentiate between an essential or unessential task. All that we do around the child is essential work!

Chapter 10
The Rhythm of the Day

Awhina is a rhythmical environment by its very nature, a therapeutic space that has been created with the child's well-being at its heart. Children are rhythmical beings who are deeply affected by the life rhythms that surround them, and naturally they are affected by the practices of the adults who care for them. Our daily rhythm supports the needs of young children. It is vitally important and needs to consistently surround the child.

The day follows a path of contraction and expansion in its movement, allowing the child to maintain a harmony of being. There is a "breathing in" with quieter activities of inside play or a story beside the fire, and a "breathing out" with song and movement and the more robust play that can happen in the garden. A rhythmical day will allow the child to go home to mother and father rested and in balance, able to make the transition happily.

The Day Begins

8:00 – 9:00 am: In the winter, the fire has been lit earlier in the morning (6:00 am), and co-workers arrive to a warmed environment, as do the children. (In the summer, the day will often begin in the garden.) As well as being warm in a physical sense, the environment is "warmed" in a soul sense through the inner preparation of the co-worker (see Appendix F). This soul warming can only come about through co-workers taking an interest not only in the children and families that come to the day nursery but also in the environment, even when it is not one's specific area of responsibility. All areas belong to all co-workers, and no one area is "owned" by any one co-worker.

It may be our task, for example, to care for the kitchen, to prepare the art and craft space, or to look to the needs of our youngest children. We do not, however own this task; rather, we own the responsibility to ensure the task is carried out well, sometimes with the contribution and assistance of other co-workers.

Subtle changes may have taken place over the weekend. Perhaps a branch has been added to the festival shelf, still reflective of winter but showing the early signs of spring blossom about to break through, placed in warm water to help the blossom to emerge. There may be a delicate movement to the first elements of spring in the coloring of the silk on the dining table, still bearing the "feel" of winter but acknowledging that spring is only around the corner. Sometimes children may notice these more subtle changes, and if they do, often no outer explanation will be uttered. They will simply take in and "bathe" in this beauty.

This taking in and bathing is a more tangible, though still unconscious, experience for the child when we adults are warmly interested in what the environment holds. In our quiet reflection and grateful observation of what has been prepared, an inner gesture of respect and love can and will pass over to the child. This, the inner work of the adult, directly relates to our work on a deeper level. In a sense we are "communing" with the world of spirit, acknowledging that all that we do could not be entered into without this spiritual guidance.

Showing interest has a warming quality that requires our constant attention. How we greet one another, in particular at the beginning of the new day, will often reflect the atmosphere of the environment and will naturally have an impact on the children in our care. The work within an anthroposophical initiative is largely to do with our inner personal journey. When this is met with a trusting gesture of honesty, then our outer work will more and more fall into place.

Children and parents arrive during the first hour of the morning. There is a gradual introduction to the Awhina day. This is a time to reconnect with the parent and to become familiar with the child's previous night.

Quiet play begins around the preparation for the day ahead. The bread dough is prepared for the morning bake. The washing is brought in from the line, folded, and ironed. All occurs with and around the children.

The hanging out of the washing is a particularly enjoyable activity for the child, especially when the caregiver carries an "inviting" gesture. The child loves to find the different colored cloths and hand them to the caregiver who hangs them on the line—all the blue cloths, all the white cloths, all the yellow cloths and so on—and the child observes it all. This is yet another opportunity for the child to experience mathematical discrimination, and what is more beautiful than to see carefully hung washing on the line? The practices of old, such as shaking out the wrinkles in the washing, thus enabling the work of folding and ironing to go more smoothly, are still true today and never more true than for the young child. Attention to detail is fast becoming something of the past, something unknown to so-called modern children.

Morning Play

By around 9:00 am most of the children have arrived and found their way to where they want to be. This is also time for the children to have a piece of fruit, usually apple, to tide them over until morning tea. The children may be in any of the following areas: the playroom, the dining room, the kitchen, or the kowhai room.

The playroom, with its rosy fire on wintry days, provides the possibility of a story on the sofa, dollies to care for, logs and building blocks and trucks and trains, house-building, and more.

The dining room is another play space, and here the work of the day continues with the caregiver. There may be fruit or vegetables to chop, mending to be done, or tables to be polished. Babies may need their first snack of the day, while at the same time little ones are also giving their dollies a snack.

The kitchen is the heart of the home and the heart of the day nursery. It is where the parents come in the morning to share the experiences of their children's previous night. It is the point of transition where the child is handed into the arms of the trusted caregiver. The kitchen often draws the children in, as a place of comfort. In the home, it is where a mother spends most of her time. It is warm, with tempting smells, tasty nibbles, dough to knead and mixtures to mix. This is a very important place for children, and for some, it provides an anchor in their early days at Awhina.

The kowhai room is a place for "doing," for all seasons. For example, in the autumn, apple rings are sliced and dried for winter sweets, and the lavender is harvested and hung to dry for use in the making of Awhina dollies. There is the possibility for crafts born out of the seasonal rhythm, such as paper lanterns for midwinter, and art activities of painting, crayoning, and so on. This room, like the others, has its own play space. Quiet spaces can always be found for a little one who simply needs a cuddle and a story. The "doing" activities are not always engaged in—rather, they are activities that are offered at different times, through careful observation of the children and the needs that manifest. For example, a child may show, through his loud and inappropriate play, that watercolor painting is what he needs: the possibility to simply flow with the water and with the color. One needs to observe the elements of watercolor painting when offered in the morning and when offered in the afternoon, and use these observations when planning.

Learning through imitation, by means of play, is how the healthy child engages. Experience shows that the children are most content in their play when the adults around them are engaged in real work. It is as if the children slip into the stream of work of the adult and in doing this, experience a warm sense of security that allows them to get on with their work and play with absolute contentment.

The adults' work may be repairing or sanding equipment, sewing blankets, repairing puppets, cleaning the windows, dusting shelves, preparing paper for painting, and so on. In the summer it is the work of the garden that calls adults and children. The interested co-worker, as she comes to know the work environment of the day nursery, will come to know what needs doing and should not have to be told. This interest fills the environment with soul warmth. The more we engage in life-filled activities, the more engaged the children will become.

Each co-worker has his or her own handwork basket, which can be taken up when

the situation allows. Children deeply connect with the experience when something is lovingly mended. They also love the magical contents that a handwork basket offers, particularly when there exists a button box or a ribbon tin within (keeping in mind the age-appropriateness of these objects). These simple but exquisite treasures feature less and less in the life of the young child. Not all co-workers are necessarily skilled at handwork, and their baskets therefore will contain other kinds of work such as wooden animals to sand or yarn to make into twisties.

The salt dough activity is brought to the children on occasion. While the kneading of bread dough is not suitable for little hands, the salt dough provides a wonderful activity for kneading, squeezing, and rolling that helps to support the little child's need to get into his body. This is entered into with only a few utensils, to allow the hands to do the work of shaping and kneading.

Care of Infants

At Awhina there are two nurseries, the Rose nursery and the Blue nursery, which are quiet and prepared spaces for our very young babies and toddlers. These spaces provide a quiet play environment for late afternoon when needed and depending on how many babies we have. (The nurseries may only be used for play when not occupied by sleeping babies.) Infants and babies are received in the morning by their caregiver in a quiet space such as the dining room or kowhai room (this needs to be consistent) to allow for a gentle transition.

Infants and babies under twelve months old are cared for by two primary caregivers, a male and a female co-worker. For some time now we have been fortunate to have a man fulfilling this important role, thus creating for the infant a balanced perception of the human being through the qualities that each gender offers. These caregivers maintain this role until the child is ready to step away. Before long the little child will come to know and trust other caregivers and will quite happily allow another to tend to her. The little one may also decide that she is intent on keeping her primary caregiver.

The two co-workers work consultatively with the parent and together decide on the right course of practice. While one is more hands-on, the other is there to offer support when needed. As babies are put down to sleep, this co-worker is free to assist where needed in other areas of Awhina.

Circle Time, Morning Tea, and Outdoor Play

Following morning play and "doing," we tidy away. Everything has a home. Each toy has its place. This is the time to work through the creative chaos. Adults and children together joyfully and playfully engage in this activity, which, if entered into in the right way, is simply an extension of the child's play. We try to make this a joyful activity in itself, and enough time should be allowed so that there is no rush.

At 9:50 am or thereabouts is a time for singing and for movement, big bodily movements and small finer movements of fingers and hands. This is the time for well-loved nursery rhymes, circle games of the seasons, a story, or perhaps a puppet play. The content and duration of this time is a reflection of the age range of the children. This should be constantly reassessed, as should the number of adults participating and the appropriateness of the very little children joining in.

When beginning a new circle time, following the puppet play, it is often supportive to begin with a well-loved nursery rhyme and add perhaps only one or two other songs or games. Build slowly, observe the children. Too much content will result in the children not being held, and they will simply move into other play that calls them more—which is acceptable, because that is what children of this age do. But then you need to ask yourself, why have a circle?

Circle time may be later in the winter and may also happen in different spaces at the same time, depending on the size of the group and the needs of the children.

10:00 am is morning tea, *Ko te wha kai* in Maori, which is a very important part of the day. The children are sung to the table that has been carefully prepared, they are seated and their hands are washed, the candle is lit, and the *karakia* (blessing) is sung. This is a moment of unconscious acknowledgment, followed by the social sharing of eating together.

Babies in high chairs need to have their food served first. They do not have the ability to wait as they see food being prepared: they see, they want—now. This slowly changes as they get older, so that the older children know that they will be served soon. The younger children have their food placed before them, rather than being given a choice, which is something they are not capable of at this age. This also takes away the element of "hers is bigger," and other conflicts. This continues until the child is around three years or older.

Following morning tea is the time for the hygienic rhythms of toileting, diaper changing, and hand washing. Although many children may have been to the toilet in the course of the morning, this provides a healthy rhythm for the child.

The youngest children are always attended to first. The co-worker will come to know which children need to go with her to the bathroom first. The children who are happily playing or helping to clear the table are able to go to the bathroom a little later. During this time two co-workers remain in the dining room, quietly clearing the table with the help of the children, or perhaps one is reading a story.

Following diaper changing and toileting, the bathrooms are tended to quickly by each co-worker. In the main bathroom the sluice basin (a separate sink for rinsing soiled cloths) will have been disinfected after each bowel motion diaper; otherwise a quick wipe around the sinks is sufficient. The diaper bin is taken out and emptied. The bathrooms will have a more thorough clean after lunch and at the end of the day.

The children now move into the garden with their caregivers. There are chickens to be fed, compost to be emptied, sandpits for digging, and the boat to be sailed, or we can simply just be in the garden.

Inside, the lunch preparation continues and the playroom is prepared for the afternoon sleep. Often the caregivers are helped by one or two children who like to be inside, either in the kitchen or helping make the beds.

The Morning Ends

11:50 am—Children and caregivers prepare to come in for lunch. The playroom has been transformed into the sleep room for the older children. Each sleeping space is prepared with care and attention to detail. Each is surrounded with a folding stand, and a sleeping dolly is there waiting for the child. The prepared space invites the child in.

Before it is time to come inside, the garden is tidied. In the winter the lower sandpit is usually tidied up for the day, though in the summer it may be available for afternoon use. When tidying the sandpit, we are re-establishing order. We also provide the children with an invitation to come into the sandpit the next day, and we indirectly also teach the children differentiation—between mixing bowls and spoons, buckets, and spades. When we mix the equipment or utensils, we provide the children with a confused picture, an untruth, and we have missed a teachable moment. The same would apply in the inside environment if the stones were to be put into the log basket, for example.

The morning comes to an end. Children who stay for the morning only have their quiet farewells. Should the parent want to discuss anything, then another time can be arranged, and this is offered in a polite and courteous manner. A warm meal is awaiting the children staying on for the afternoon. These children are received by the inside co-worker. This is an important transition for the children, who are often tired as well as hungry, and it needs to be treated with the utmost care.

Lunch and Rest Time

Babies are fed by the caregiver on the knee until such time as the little one is able to sit independently. The children under two years of age are assisted in their feeding—where necessary, two spoons are used, allowing the child a sense of autonomy while at the same time ensuring that they are getting enough to eat.

Toileting as well as the cleaning of teeth follows the meal. Each child has his or her own tooth brush, toothpaste, and mug. The caregiver cleans the child's teeth. The child assists by holding the mug in which there is a little rinsing water, and afterwards drying the mug.

Soon the day nursery is resting. For caregivers, there is a cup of tea, with time to reflect on the children and the morning. Children who are not sleeping are carried consciously by one or more co-workers. This resting time needs to be planned for, just as other areas of the day are planned for. It is considered a quiet play time, a time for the child to replenish life forces.

Guiding Baby to Sleep

Sleep is important for infants and little children. It is the time when they rest from the world, from being social, to replenish and to grow. A healthy restful sleep will depend on the soul/spiritual space of the caregiver and his or her attention and care when preparing baby and the physical space of the nursery for sleep.

Baby will be ready for sleep because her individual rhythm indicates this, but there are other signs we need to become aware of that will show us this little one may need to go the bed earlier or more frequently. Gaining a comprehensive picture of the previous night from the parent is essential. This may reveal that the baby has had an unsettled night or has woken earlier than usual. Baby may have the beginnings of a cold, or she may be teething. These are all indications that her sleep rhythms may require closer attention.

Sleep is a comforting and soothing respite, giving the child the sanctuary that is so needed for very young children through the day, especially in the day nursery environment. When a little one is unwell, be it teething or a cold or sometimes both, then the comfort of their prepared sleeping space is what is needed at this time.

To support the child in the best possible way requires a preparation on two levels, the inner and the outer. A "centering" is necessary if we are to be fully with the baby in our preparations. This will support the little one into sleep. During this time of preparing for sleep, know that this is what you are doing and that any other happenings around you will be attended to by other co-workers. This then implies that other co-workers are aware of what you are doing and respect this moment in time. Everyone benefits because baby will sleep better as a result of your attention. Your thoughts center around baby, your gestures are soothing and comforting. Baby knows that you are there for her alone; your very gestures will express this. Remember that from the moment you begin this task, your thoughts turn to a "right" attitude of being with this little one. My picture has always been that of the child's guardian angel standing behind the child.

The outer preparation involves all that is needed in the way of the physical needs: diaper care, warming and tidying the sleeping space, making sure that baby's sleeping dolly is in the cot, and so on.

The nursery should be warm and aired. It is important that as baby awakes from sleep that the curtains are pulled back, allowing sunlight and air to fill and cleanse, so to speak, the nursery, in preparation for another child who may be going to bed soon.

Before you place baby on the changing table, know that you have all that you need at hand. Removing the diaper (disposable) should be done with the utmost care when opening the side tabs. A very rough sound is made when this is done quickly and will startle baby.

If a chest rub is used, your hands need to be warm. If your hands are cold, this not only startles or shocks baby, it will awaken her. Never leave baby exposed without any covering—this is where a wrap can be used to drape over or around baby. The younger the baby the more I maintain physical contact, as with the palm of my hand on the baby's belly providing both warmth and a feeling of being secure.

With the diaper in place and any medicaments applied, baby is then snugly enfolded in her own wrap, leaving the arms free. The wrapping of baby is a twofold gesture. First, the wrap is almost like another skin and so acts as a form of protection, of security, something our modern children need. Second, we "embrace" baby with our own gesture of soul warmth—enfolding the child with our being, with our presence that remains with the infant long after she is asleep.

I tell baby quietly that it is her bedtime, not engaging in eye contact, and then singing the Awhina lullaby. Baby is carried in the horizontal quietly to her nursery. I have always stood at the window quietly saying "goodnight" to the garden and to the chickens, pulling the curtains and then placing the little one in her cot. If baby has not already reached for her sleeping dolly then this is handed to her.

Baby and sleeping dolly are tucked in securely, in the winter with the woolen duvet and a light woolen blanket (if necessary) and in the summer, a fine cotton sheet and light wool blanket if necessary. If a heater has been on to warm the nursery, it is turned off before leaving the nursery.

The Afternoon

There are three co-workers (sometimes four, depending on the number of children) in the afternoon. One or two will be gently awakening the children, one is in the garden, and the third or fourth co-worker, whom we call the "floater," clears the dishwasher, prepares the afternoon tea, and is there to assist indoors or out. When the balance of children moves into the garden, this co-worker joins everyone outside.

When time allows, the preparation of the sauce for the next day may be started, and children love to assist with the chopping of the softer vegetables. Naturally, the presence of babies will require a different working depending on what the needs are.

The children, well rested after their lunch, have a different approach to play

than they do in the morning, and this needs to be acknowledged when planning the afternoon rhythm. Observe where the children like to be. Where is the warmest or coolest part of the garden, depending on the season? Remember that when the co-worker is engaged in "real" work, then so too will be the children.

Afternoon Tasks

The sleep room is tidied away as each child awakes: the child, with caregiver, puts the sleeping dolly in his bag, and the sheet and blanket are folded and put away in their appointed place. The sleeping corner is tidied away and playthings returned to their rightful homes. The caregiver and child put the mattress away, and together they go to the bathroom.

With the rising of the last child, the playroom is in order for the next day. This is done with no rush, always allowing for the children to awaken in their own time and in their own way. Those children who are slow to wake are able to hear the activity of the children quietly getting up and slowly come to a point of wakefulness that will allow them to leave their bed at the right time.

When a nursery baby awakens at around the same time, then the nursery door is opened, (with the caregiver giving assurance to the little one that she will be there soon). Nursery babies do not need to be taken up from their bed the moment they awake. Through consistency of practice they come to know and to trust that the caregivers will be with them soon. The door is opened and the little one can hear the voice of the caregiver, sometimes singing and sometimes in quiet conversation with a child, and will happily play in the cot until he or she appears. The nursery is a beautiful and carefully prepared space for the baby, and this time in the cot allows the little one to experience this space.

This may be a new experience for babies who have been responded to with every sound that they make. These babies will need time to adjust. However, with consideration by the caregiver, careful consultation with the parent (if needed), and consistency of practice, these babies will find their new rhythm.

By 2:30 – 3:00 pm the children are awake and well rested. It is afternoon tea time.

The inside co-worker will have all inside tasks completed by 3:00 pm or thereabouts. This means moving through each room to check that all is in place, in particular any toys from the morning that may have found their way into a different room. Firewood (in the winter months) is brought in by a free co-worker, assisted by one or two children.

If and when toys or equipment are not returned to their rightful home, then it is important to let co-workers know the next day. It may be that the co-worker does not know where specific toys live. When everything is where it should be, we surround the child with the security of knowing that there is a home for everything and everything has a home.

3:30 pm—The last task for the inside co-worker is to ensure each bathroom is cleaned. All inside tasks are complete. The chickens are fed and housed, the sandpits are raked and watered, the washing is hung out (if not hung out in the morning) and the bread dough (for overnight rising) is put to bed.

4:30 pm—The final task of the last co-worker is to walk through the day nursery ensuring that all is in place and that the curtains are closed in the winter. The last co-worker is ready to leave soon after the last child has gone home.

Co-workers, especially those at Awhina all day, are encouraged to find moments through the day where a breath can be taken with a drink or cup of tea. There may be children around; however, in your gesture of "a quiet moment" the children will usually oblige with a similar gesture or contentedly play around you. Five or ten minutes of respite dotted through the day can do wonders for one's energy levels.

Chapter 11
Planning a Menu
for the Day Nursery

The menu in the day nursery is based on the main grain varieties—wheat, rice, barley, millet, rye, oats, and to a lesser extent sweet corn (only used fresh when in season in late summer)—as well as fresh fruit, herbs, and vegetables, including produce from the biodynamic day nursery garden. All foods are from Demeter or certified organic sources wherever possible.

Wheat, barley, rye, and oats are used in the Zentrofan four-grain flour. This is milled by a process that involves the grain being blown against a stone, which produces a fine flour with superior nutritional qualities and lighter baking properties than a regular grinding mill. It is used for all the baking requirements within the day nursery.

Additionally, whole grains are cooked on the corresponding days of the week: rice on Monday, barley on Tuesday, millet on Wednesday, oats on Friday. On Thursday, rye is used in the form of crackers for morning tea; whole rye grain is possibly too heavy for young children. The children become familiar with the menu and eagerly look forward to the meal on any given day. The children name the days of the week by the day's meal,—millet day instead of Wednesday—which is appropriate to the consciousness of the young child.

The three different groups of vegetables—root, leaf, and flower/fruit—are used in every meal to ensure a nutritional balance is achieved, hence supporting the nerve/sense, rhythmical, and limb/metabolic systems respectively.[44]

The typical daily meal times are "fruit time" at 9 am, morning tea at 10 am, lunch at noon, and afternoon tea at 3 pm.

Sample Menus

Fruit time: Apples or other fruit in season.

Morning Tea: See daily changes below.

Lunch: See daily changes below.

Afternoon tea: either leftover bread from the morning or crackers with almond butter, fresh and dried fruit, nuts, and herbal tea or water.

Monday:

Morning tea: four-grain bread with butter, yeast spread,[45] and avocado, and fresh fruit. Herbal tea, using herbs from the garden.

Lunch: Rice risotto with herbs and vegetables, e.g. carrots, silver beet (Swiss chard), pumpkin, and cauliflower. Water.

Tuesday:

Morning tea: Four-grain bread/rolls with butter, yeast spread, and avocado, and fresh fruit. Herbal tea.

Lunch: Barley stew with herbs and vegetables, e.g. carrots, silver beet, pumpkin, and broccoli. Water.

Wednesday:

Morning tea: Four grain bread/rolls with almond butter, fresh fruit. Herbal tea.

Lunch: Millet with herbs and vegetables, e.g. carrots, silver beet, pumpkin, and beetroot. Water.

---

44   Rudolf Steiner, *Nutrition and Health,* 4ff.

45   Almond or hazelnut butter may be substituted for yeast spread, a favorite in New Zealand but not always readily available elsewhere.

Thursday:

Morning tea: Rye crackers with almond butter, fresh fruit. Herbal tea.

Lunch:

Summer—pizza with tomato and grated carrot and silver beet or spinach, topped with feta or mozzarella and grated edam cheese. Water.

Winter—whole grain kamut (or wheat) pasta with sweet potato (kumera) sauce including silver beet and pumpkin. Water.

Friday:

Morning tea: Waffles with butter and homemade jam. Herbal tea.

Lunch:

Summer—Bircher Muesli. Water.

Winter—Apple crumble with cornmeal custard. Water.

During the course of the year there are seasonal and festival-related variations at morning tea time. For example, on Shrove Tuesday pancakes are prepared, including the ritual of "tossing" the pancake, hot cross buns are baked during Holy Week, and star biscuits are prepared with the children during Advent, as are shortbread dove biscuits at Whitsun. A simple cake is baked by the parent for the birthday celebration.

Recipes

Except as noted, the quantities indicated serve around 12 children and 4 adults.

Herbal tea:

Pick fresh herbs such as lemon balm, lemon verbena, or pineapple sage, depending on what is available. Steep in hot water, and add to lukewarm water.[46] All teas are served warm, to support the child's digestion.

Bread:

The bread dough is mixed the previous night and is the last activity in the day nursery for the day.

Mix 750 grams (6 cups) of four-grain flour and a pinch of salt with lukewarm water, including dissolved yeast to make a moist, but not wet, mixture.

By allowing the dough to rise overnight, the amount of yeast can be dramatically reduced to as little as 5 grains of dried yeast in the summer and a little more in the winter.

---

46   Michaela Glöckler, *Guide to Child Health*, 249.

Keep bowl warm by covering it with a plastic hat and tucking it into a woolen blanket bed made of a cotton pillowcase (separate for easy washing) which slides into an outer woolen envelope made from a thick woolen blanket.

The next morning, punch down the dough. Grease two bread pans and fill 3/4 full with the dough. Allow dough to rise until ready to bake (when dough has reached top of form and is slightly domed). This takes approximately 45–60 minutes. Bake at 180 degrees centigrade (350 Fahrenheit) for 50–60 minutes.

When making bread rolls, use the same dough preparation as for bread. Add flour to make a firmer dough and form rolls, letting them rise on a greased baking sheet. Bake for 12–15 minutes.

This is a basic recipe, and as with all things, one forms a relationship to the dough, especially when preparing it daily. You come to know just how much water is needed, and other nuances related to the substance. While most co-workers at some time or other prepare the dough for the bread, it is interesting to note that each co-worker's bread will have its own quality and none will be exactly alike.

Waffles:

Mix 3 bantam eggs[47] or 2 regular eggs with 1/4 cup of unrefined sugar and a few drops of pure almond essence. Mix well until sugar is dissolved. Warm 1 liter (4 cups) of milk and 50 grams (4 tablespoons) of butter, add a teaspoon of yeast, and let it sit for 5 to 10 minutes. Add this to the egg mixture and mix well. Add approximately 500 grams (4 cups) of four-grain flour, mix well, and let rest for 20–30 minutes.

The mixture should be of a thick but runny consistency. Bake waffles in waffle iron until golden brown. When brought to the table they do not last long! Makes enough for twenty hungry children and five adults, and sometimes there are some left for afternoon tea!

Risotto:

Soak 2 cups of whole brown rice overnight. In the morning drain the rice, put it into an ovenproof dish, and warm the grain at 50 degrees centigrade (100 degrees Fahrenheit) for 20–30 minutes to "open" the grain.

Sauté one small onion and a clove of garlic, diced carrots, silver beet, and pieces of pumpkin, add the rice, and stir for 5 minutes. Add herbs from the garden.

Add several cups of water to cover and cook on a slow simmer for around 45 minutes. Check water level regularly and add water to prevent sticking.

---

47   Michaela Glöckler, *Guide to Child Health*, 256 ff.

Steam or boil cauliflower and serve as a side dish, toss with herbs and a little olive oil just before serving.

Barley Stew:

Soak 2 cups of barley overnight. In the morning drain the barley, put it into an ovenproof dish, and warm the grain at 50 degrees centigrade (100 degrees Fahrenheit) for 20–30 minutes to "open" the grain.

Sauté one small onion and a clove of garlic, carrot rounds, silver beet, and pieces of pumpkin, add the barley and stir for 5 minutes. Add seasonal herbs.

Add several cups of water, cover, and simmer for 45 minutes. Check water level regularly to prevent sticking, and add more if needed. Barley requires more water than rice. Steam or boil broccoli and serve as a side dish.

Millet:

Sauté a small onion and a clove of garlic, shaved carrots, silver beet or other green vegetable, pumpkin, and herbs. Add a little water and simmer for 30 minutes to make the sauce.

Bring 5–6 cups of water to boil, add 2 cups of hulled millet, and simmer until the water has disappeared. Take off the heat and mix in a tablespoon of organic extra virgin olive oil.

Watch that the millet does not stick!

Cook 2 or 3 whole beetroots, drain, and dice when cooled. Serve as a side dish.

Awhina Pizza:

Prepare dough as in bread recipe. Next morning, punch down the dough, add a little more flour to make a firmer dough, and allow it to rise again.

Oil two baking sheets well and with the heel of the hand, using a little extra oil if needed, press the dough out until trays are covered. Spread the dough sparingly with cooked, cooled tomato sauce. (For sauce: sauté 1 small onion and 1 clove of garlic in 2 teaspoons of olive oil, add 1 can of organic tomatoes[48] and fresh basil, marjoram, or thyme. Cook to reduce the sauce until almost all moisture has evaporated.) Sprinkle with mozzarella or feta cheese sparingly and a small amount of grated Edam cheese.

Bake in a hot oven (210 degrees centigrade/425 degrees Fahrenheit) for 10–15 minutes. Let cool before cutting and serving.

---

48   Michaela Glöckler, *Guide to Child Health*, 249.

Pasta:

Simmer cut sweet potatoes (not potato),[49] silver beet, seasonal herbs, and diced pumpkin until soft. Using the vegetable water, mash the sweet potato, adding a tablespoon of olive oil. Cook 500 grams (one pound) of whole grain pasta until reasonably soft. Serve pasta and sauce topped with a light sprinkling of feta.

Vegetables given here are only indicative. Use whatever is in season or available, but ensure that all three groups are covered. Softer green leafy vegetables, such as silver beet, need to be added later in the cooking process.

Awhina Muesli:

To 1 kg (2 pounds) of rolled oats add 2 cups of shredded coconut, 1/2 cup sunflower seeds, and 1/2 cup of other chopped nuts such as walnuts, hazelnuts, or almonds, and mix well.

Heat (do not allow to come to boil) 1/2 cup of olive oil and 2 tablespoons of honey. Add to the oat mixture and mix well with two forks.

Bake in slow oven (90–100 degrees centigrade/200 degrees Fahrenheit), turning often until golden and crisp.

Add dried fruit to taste such as sultanas, apricots, or dates when the muesli has cooled.

Store in airtight jars.

Bircher Muesli:

Fill a large bowl with Awhina muesli and add 2 freshly grated apples and 3 cooked apples. Pour on approximately 1/2 liter (1 pint) of milk and leave overnight in refrigerator. Bring to room temperature and add yogurt and a little honey or maple syrup before serving.

Apple Crumble:

Stew 2–3 kg (4–6 lbs) of apples. Place in an ovenproof dish. Top with Awhina muesli and keep warm in the oven at a low temperature.

Make custard by dissolving 3 tablespoons of cornmeal in cold milk, which is then stirred into 1/2 liter (1 pint) of hot milk. Slightly sweeten with honey or maple syrup.

Stir continuously until the custard thickens. It sticks very easily.

---

49   Michaela Glöckler, *Guide to Child Health*, 251.

Hot Cross Buns:

This is a great recipe and never fails. Don't make the dough too firm—it needs to feel light in texture.

Into a warm bowl place 500 grams (1 lb) organic white flour, salt, 1 teaspoon cinnamon, 2 oz each of currants and raisins, and mix. (We use organic white flour for festival bakings, as this brings something different and adds a quality of lightness that is reflective of a festival mood.)

Warm 1/2 pint milk, dissolve 2 tablespoons granulated sugar in this and sprinkle 3/4 oz yeast on top, leave for 10 minutes until spongy.

Pour yeast mixture into center of flour mix and make a soft dough; knead for 5–10 minutes.

Oil bowl, place kneaded dough in bowl, cover, and leave to double in size.

Punch down the dough, knead just a little, divide into small portions, and place on greased tray. Cover with a cloth, allow to double in size in a warm, draft-free place, for around 40 minutes.

Place a cross on each bun, made of a paste of flour, oil, and water. I like to add a little almond essence as well. Knead and roll out small pieces between hands.

Bake in a hot oven, around 200 degrees centigrade (400 degrees Fahrenheit) for about 15 minutes. Check the temperature of your oven! 🏠

Chapter 12
The Child's Relationship to the Doll

There is nothing more sacred than making a doll for a beloved child. The creating, which may be experienced as an "ensouling," begins with the first piece of fleece that is taken to begin rolling the head, organically building up, little by little, each layer of wool...a gesture of enfolding, of wrapping, until you have before you a beautiful sphere. For the young child, this sphere, which is later to become the head of the dolly, resonates of cosmic memories.

The loving gestures we use will "sing" to the child, who experiences them in every fold and every nuance of the dolly. The soul life of the very young child lives between two worlds, the spiritual and the earthly world, with the little child and his day-dreaming still passing lightly to and fro from one paradise to another—heaven and earth are one.

The Child's First Doll

The little child's first doll—I call it the sleeping dolly—is but a reflection of this cosmic realm and supports the little one as mediator between these two realms. The sleeping dolly, the simplest of dolls, accompanies the little child as she "sleeps" her way into earthly life.

One has only to watch the little baby having recently woken and at just six months able to take hold of her little sleeping dolly. First the baby's hand comes to rest on something that is already becoming a part of her. The little hand closes around the soft, wooly bundle and immediately lifts this to the mouth and nose, literally "tasting" the dolly and then holding it slightly away and simply breathing her in. I have spent many a moment in awe of the special quality of this moment. The baby of six months is "here" in that she is awake (from her sleep) but in her "dreaming" oblivious to anything in her nursery other than her dolly, which is simply a bundle of fleece and wool, lovingly fashioned in a simple way to imbue the qualities of the human being.

The Sleeping Dolly

Just as the young child lives in transition between the world of spirit and the earthly realm, it is the sleeping dolly who supports the daily transition from home to the day nursery and from day nursery to home again. Just as the child and family become a part of the day nursery environment so too does the sleeping dolly become part of the child's home.

In the early days of the day nursery, we found that many children liked to bring an array of soft toys with them. We simply asked that home toys stay at home and introduced the sleeping dolly, which was for sleep time only and which would go home with the child each day.

These dollies are very simple. However, to make a soft dolly with the child in mind carries with it certain responsibilities. We need to carry an inner picture of the "uprightness" of the human being, as well as an outer observation of the healthy physical being.

The sleeping dolly is made in what has been described as a "meditation in doing," carrying an inner picture of the child. It is with this attention to detail that the sleeping dolly is ensouled, and which enables the child to so readily take hold of this dolly. The quality of a harmonious whole is reflected in the composition of the dolly, made from just one piece of fabric, and this in turn accompanies the child, who lives in a state of consciousness described as a "sleeping" or "mono-consciousness," which expresses the child's "at-oneness" with his environment.

Making a dolly is one of the greatest gifts we can offer the child, for it is in crafting the soft toy, with care and in a right process, that we ensoul the dolly with an inner gesture. It is this soul gesture that the child connects with. The dolly is imbued with dried lavender, surrounding the child with a quality of harmony and peace. Where possible, Awhina dollies are made from natural fabrics and materials that have been salvaged or recycled. This provides an "enduring" soul quality to the finished doll.

In the morning, the parent with the child carefully places sleeping dolly in the child's cot (for the baby) or the basket in the playroom (for the older child).

Occasionally parents are reminded that the gesture of respect and care that they give to the sleeping dolly will also be reflected in the gestures of the child. Parents are asked not to underestimate the significance of this special dolly to the child, which offers a unique bond that links the day nursery and home. When the parent handles this dolly with a genuine warmth and love, the child too is warmed by this loving gesture.

The sleeping dolly is for that sacred time of the day and night when the child reconnects with her spiritual origins. Dolly is there when the child drifts into sleep and dolly is there when the child reawakens to the world. It is just that, a dolly for sleeping. There are other dolls that the child has for play. This dolly, however, has a particular role in the child's soul life.

Doll Play for Older Children

Daniel Udo De Haes[50] describes the little child as not yet having any conscious picture of the human being, but says that in his soul this concept lives as a foundation of his development. The child's soul continues to be vividly animated by an archetypal idea of humanity, and from it he begins and continues to fashion his life.

Little children, in their play, practice themselves into life. They re-enact the adult world of relationships in miniature. They learn little by little to become social, mainly by imitating those adults who are around them the most.

Children come to an experience of "self" in their relationship with others—surrounded by adults, sharing healthy and loving relationships. It is natural for the child to imitate warmth expressed by the other. The outpouring of love is intensely felt in the whole being of the child—a two-year-old will, without any apparent motive, approach another, enfolding this child in her embrace. The joy experienced by all is so very tangible. The "need" to nurture the dolly, which arises primarily out of imitation, is also somehow an innate instinct in the healthy child and yet another reason to support children being in mixed-age groups.

At Awhina, play and dolls and the day in the life of the child are one. An environment where dolls are loved and respectfully cared for has very consciously been developed. Each dolly has a cradle with its own blankets and one or two even have little sleeping dollies. The dolls have become a part of the life of the children.

No house built would be complete without one or two (sometimes more) "babies" to care for. Often a highchair will be brought to the morning tea table—complete with a bib and a drinking cup—not for one of our Awhina toddlers, but for a dolly! The child does not distinguish between what is play and what is real, because they are one and

---

50   Daniel Udo De Haes, *The Young Child*, 25.

the same. The child totally, and with his whole being, embraces the dolly and cares for it, his soul experiencing the image of the human being. With this unconscious yet profound experience, the child's journey into life and further development is strengthened and deepened.

Above all, the doll provides the possibility for the child to be supported in his need to become, to enter the world of relationship that begins with mother and father, brother and sister. The doll has the potential to become the child's first special friend because hidden from the unseeing eye of the adult are archetypal mysteries, so tangible to the child and his dreaming world of heaven and earth.

The Awhina dolls have been created with this cosmic picture in mind. On the one hand, the doll, a representative of the human being displaying healthy human qualities, supports the little child into the upright. It goes without saying that in making the doll we carry in mind a picture of the healthy human being with well-proportioned features. On the other hand, the doll imbues the child with cosmic memories, leaving him dreamily "absorbed" in the spiritual origin of mankind. These memories and recollections naturally live unconsciously in the little child, but manifest outwardly as a sense of comfort and security.

When making a doll, we need to learn to observe and in our own development learn to be self-critical. We must aspire to the best for our young children and sometimes this will mean re-doing again and again and maybe even again, remembering that the child will love and respect his doll as much as we love and respect his doll. ▣

Chapter 13
Indoor Activities

The Toddler in the Family Group Setting

Looking at the facilities and spaces that we have, how can we be creative and find a good way of managing when we need to be indoors, in particular with our toddlers and little ones aged around eighteen to twenty-one months?

For the child to call to life all the good that he brings with him from his heavenly home, and for these gifts to thrive, depends not only on our loving and understanding care, but in large measure also on the quality of the surroundings in which he grows up.[51]

Children at this age are very "egocentric." They are only just at the beginning of playing with one another and in general are completely self-centered. "Me," "mine," and "me want" are frequently heard. Questions to ask are: Is the playroom actually suitable for this age or is it too large? What is it that children at this age need?

The child around twenty months needs space, but with certain confines and boundaries. He needs the presence of an attentive but active adult who may be doing simple, meaningful tasks, around and near the child. It may be wiping down the shelves, or it may be cleaning the inside of the windows. This work takes hold of the child, motivating him to become engaged in the gesture of the adults' work through play. The caregiver therefore needs to be prepared with extra cloths and aprons for the many helpers who, with joy, will want to be involved as well.

---

51   Daniel Udo de Haes, *The Young Child*, 22.

The child senses through our mood, through our relationship to what we are doing (no word needs to be spoken), how we live and connect with that which surrounds us. The young child is searching for an entrance to the earthly world through his "breathing in" of his environment. This is strengthened and guided through our connection to and penetration of the environment and the tasks we engage in.

It is not our right to force our sympathy on the child; rather, it is through a right intention in our doing that we guide the child into those experiences that live as a cosmic memory and now take on a more conscious form—the gentle flow of water, the care of the dolly, a butterfly weaving its way, the tending of nature's garden, a gentle shower of rain. We take these aspects of everyday life for granted, but for the sake of the child we need to begin to see and experience with new eyes, in a modest but very real way. It is through our reconnecting with these everyday events and the joy that can be found in this that we support the child to fully enter and find his way into his earthly home.

The children under two-and-a-half need to be (for want of a better word) "distributed" through the day nursery when inside. Being with their peers poses all kinds of threats, and I do not believe this is supportive given the ego nature of this age. Being in a small group of varying ages, or with an adult who is caring for an infant, can be very supportive and affirming for the very young child.

The attention and empathy of the caregiver are often called upon. We need to be present not just physically, but in the way a mother would be present around such little ones. We need to be there with the right consciousness and with a warm objectivity.

The playroom is for creative doing when the child finds the means to play—when the need to play emerges from within, a natural development in the healthy child. Through imitation he wants and needs to construct, to create, to build. These children, from around two-and-a-half years old onward, should be allowed this opportunity without interference from the younger child. This is not to say that from time to time, the younger child cannot be invited to become part of the play of the three- or four-year-old, to the delight of all. What this does imply is that the caregiver is intimately aware of the needs of the children in their different stages of development and looks to meeting these needs in a creative and harmonious way.

Being Creative on a Wet Day

On a wet day, we might use the kowhai room as a play space until after morning tea, with the tables being pushed aside or even removed if necessary. Following morning tea, painting or another craft activity can be prepared for. The play space is still there, but a new possibility is being offered. The caregiver needs to be prepared, to have something up her sleeve, so to speak, for a wet day, remembering always the age of the child.

It is important to realize that when a large group of children are inside for a longer period of time, then the type of energy required to simply "be" is far greater. Some children may not have that energy and need to be surrounded with caring adults. One needs to come to know those children who do not manage well and make good use of the different play spaces available, remembering that little children are more supported in small groups.

There is always the possibility of the covered verandah where two or three little ones can be with a caregiver, sweeping, tidying, or bringing in the washing. Having too many children out on the verandah will defeat the purpose of what you are doing and why; decide what is the number you can happily cope with and quietly go.

Learn to observe the child: is he uncomfortable, does he throw toys, is he trying to tell us something? The only way a child (before the acquisition of language) can tell us that something is not right, is through his actions, through his state of well-being! Some children have "large" etheric/life bodies and find it very difficult to be in confined spaces with many others for any length of time—they literally bump into others without actually physically touching, and they cannot bear this.

A walk in the garden with two or three children, well clothed against the elements, perhaps just to say hello to the chickens or to gather some herbs for the kitchen, can change a dynamic and engage a little excess energy and can be a breath of fresh air for all, children and caregivers alike.

Have on hand a resource file for appropriate "doing" or age-appropriate play, that could assist you on an inside day, for example:

▲   A specially prepared mini circle leading into a simple puppet play story.

▲   Little children love nursery rhymes; find or make your own special nursery rhyme book that you bring out just occasionally.

▲   Make simple dollies from wool fleece or other material that are finished quickly and that the children can play with.

▲   Have an ongoing project that the children connect with whenever you bring out your basket—this may be something for the doll's house or for a cradle, something that the child can form a connection to.

▲   Painting can be very therapeutic for those children who cannot seem to find a connection with anything.

Make use of the various play spaces, thus keeping the groups of children in any one space small. For example, with twenty children and five co-workers and four play spaces, one would look to have around five children in each space.

The Picture Book

Sharing the right book with a child can be the perfect activity for a quiet time indoors. The following words by Daniel Udo de Haes give a beautiful picture of the many dynamics and qualities involved in the simple act of reading to the child.

When we look quietly at a picture book with a child, we can in the most natural and unforced way combine image, movement, sound, facial expression and whatever else, in a harmonious whole. This is of course of the greatest importance for the connection between the "language of things" and our "spoken language."

The picture book has another quality which can be of particular importance. Through it, all that has approached the child, is brought to him and speaks to him anew in the language of pictures, but now, as expressed by human beings.This is akin to the way a painter can teach us to "see" something, for instance through a beautiful landscape: we see it through him and with him. The child now sees and feels that he does not stand alone in his meetings and experiences with his surroundings. He will feel welcomed and understood by us, through

looking at a picture book, for he tries to become still more strongly aware of the adult's sense of oneness with his world. With this in mind, there should be no reason whatsoever to think that dwelling upon the most normal everyday things should have a narrowing or trivializing effect. On the contrary, we saw that it is just these "normal" things which have the greatest and most important messages to impart, for they bring to expression the simplest and most fundamental aspects of life on earth.[52]

Choose a selection of books for this age which are aesthetically pleasing, preferably with only one image per page. Have them prepared before you have need of them. Know what you want for the little child. Find a movement through the seasons that "walks" the child in a natural way through the year. Take responsibility for the books that are kept in the cupboard. Bring books that you want to use to the pedagogical meeting and talk about your reasons for choosing them.

Developmentally Appropriate Activities

We need to surround ourselves with a deeper understanding of the two-year-old and just where he stands on his incarnating journey into the earthly realm.

Our focus is in supporting the child's journey of unfolding. both from a spiritual aspect, which involves our inner work and study, and from a physical aspect, which involves the preparation of the environment in an appropriate and caring manner.

Thus if the child is utterly and spontaneously absorbed in his play, obviously he should be left undisturbed; whereas if a child can play only with great difficulty, it can sometimes work beneficially if we join him. (This is particularly true of the very young children.)

A large part of the child's play consists of imitation: mother carrying baby in her arms and caring for it, father doing something in the garden and so forth. But what is there for the child to truly imitate if the adult takes a doll in his arms or hammers with a toy hammer? We are clearly concerned here with a different kind of encouragement from the deliberate example given in the course of play. Sitting together on chairs and making the sounds of a cart or a train in a tunnel, will be more effectual. The same goes for floating a little boat on the water, building a little house together out of blocks and so on.

---

52   Daniel Udo de Haes, *The Young Child*, 62ff.

Even when we do not participate in or encourage his play, our interest in the child is vital. In play, the heavenly aspect of the child's being unites with the earthly world; and if we have an open eye and an open heart for this, the child feels it, and this is to him a comparison that brings confidence to help him on his way.[53]

Bearing in mind the young age of the child, our aim is not to provide activities as such, but rather to be engaged in a worthy "doing" when with the child. The domestic activities are immensely right for the young child. The stirring of the mixture or dough, the forming and molding of dough call forth good bodily movements in the child.[54]

The well-being of the young child is directly related to the physical, for example in regard to warmth and food. Cast your mind back, if you can, to baking with mother and the most favorite part: licking the bowl afterwards. Chopping the fruit or soft vegetables, any food preparation that can be done around and with the child should be done in this way. When it is fruit time, note how the little ones simply gather around.

Little children love games; peek-a-boo, building up, and knocking down bring unceasing pleasure, as do lap games accompanied with singing. Each co-worker could have a special body or lap game that the child comes to know and love and asks for over and over again.

Finger games, songs, and nursery rhymes are the eternal favorites. They are most appropriate given their rhythm, simplicity, and archetypal pictures that speak directly to the young child. Finger games for the very young child should try to call the whole body into play rather than just the fingertips. This has a more rounded, whole quality and is less awakening. The child experiences throughout his entire body.

De Haes expresses eloquently the young child's relationship to language:

The child longs to hear the mystery of human speech. Together with what his surroundings speak to him, he can experience the unity formed by these two aspects of his experience. We should—without disturbing what the child himself perceives—allow him at suitable moments to hear our human words, so that these may join in an intimate dialogue with the language of his surroundings. The point here is that both our human language and the silent language of things proceed from the same inaudible heavenly world and therefore they should develop together. If we have such an awareness, it can work in a helpful way for the toddler.

---

53   Daniel Udo de Haes, *The Young Child*, 58.

54   Audrey E. McAllen, *Sleep*, 26.

To take the example of water running into a bowl, we should let this gushing speak so that the child can take in that language in all its purity and recognize it inwardly. Then without making too much of it, we can at another time let him hear clearly the sh sound and the word gush. The child can then experience the extent to which the human being even in his language carries the whole world within him and is himself a microcosm of the world. When we are walking in the garden and then speak the word tree and maybe also the word rustling, the child will find a proper connection with this only if in these sounds he hears something of what the rustling tree has first spoken to him.

In this way it is possible for the child to experience through our words, an inner connection between the language of things and human language.[55]

Allow the child to be part of your work—when attending to an infant, for example, allow the toddler or young child to stand on a stool in order to be part of what you are doing. While your attention is with the infant, your warming interest will embrace the young child watching you, also attentively. Your soothing voice washes over the young child, as it does the infant.

Our work is twofold: *caring* for the infant or toddler on the one hand, and *doing.* This we try to do in a way that supports the watching child and allows for play through the imitation of worthy role-modeling. While caring for the environment, always be aware of little ones around you by having extra cloths handy when the child sees that you are wiping or dusting shelves. They will want, and in fact, will need to be involved as well.

The need for a quiet preparedness both internally and externally cannot be overly stressed. All we have discussed we could call "creative doing," which engages the young child in a totally unconscious way appropriate to the age and stage of development.

The Puppet Play for Little Children

The very first story that the child hears comes from the mother, and may be in the form of a lullaby. The sound of mother's voice gently awakens the child and yet still allows for the child to experience the wholeness, the sense of oneness that is so much a picture of the little child and his environment. In the day nursery, we support this at-oneness or "sleeping consciousness," this quality of wholeness, in a number of ways.

---

55   Daniel Udo de Haes, *The Young Child*, 60.

We do this by using the third person voice (I refer to myself by name rather than using "I" and I address the child by using her name rather than using "you"), by not raising our voice to the child, and by means of the stories we bring to the child. These will be simple little stories about the child's day, or they may be in the form of a puppet play.

At Awhina we bring the same beloved puppet plays year after year. In doing so, the children come to know, love, and anticipate them. The puppet play accompanies the children for around three weeks, sometimes longer. They carry a simple story line that bears within it a symbolic picture—for instance, "The Giant Turnip," where good human qualities exist. Most of the puppet plays we bring have a repetitive quality with a sung refrain, which especially appeals to young children.

The puppet play is prepared by a co-worker for some time before it is shown to the children. The key to bringing the children with you right into the puppet play is preparation. The puppeteer's role is that of moving the puppets and of telling the story. The puppeteer's consciousness breathes into the puppet play and travels as far as the periphery of the cloth or veil. Beyond this point is the concern or realm of the other co-workers.

To maintain a sense of oneness, we need to ensure that the cloths are wrinkle-free and are of colors that support the story. There is a vast difference in the experience of a beautifully ironed cloth and one that is taken out of the basket and used as is. The puppeteer endeavors also to be wearing a color that simply becomes part of the scenery, allowing for the child to become one with the mood of the moment.

How the puppets are moved will have a profound effect on the children, as they will take the story back into their own playing. Is the puppet bumped along, or is it moved along as a picture of the human qualities of walking? Whatever we present to the children must be brought with truth and not in any way be caricatured or misrepresented. Just as important is how we handle the puppet. We take hold of the shoulders of the puppet rather than the head, for the head is a sacred part of the human body and should be respected as such.

For the very young child, the best stage for the puppet play is the body or the floor. In using our body we offer something of ourselves, and sometimes this is not easy. The floor is a wonderful stage. It provides much scope. The children are one with you and can participate easily, and it is natural that creative play should develop from this. Children are often on the floor, and on the floor you can be anywhere and everywhere. ▣

Chapter 14
Seasonal and Festival Celebrations

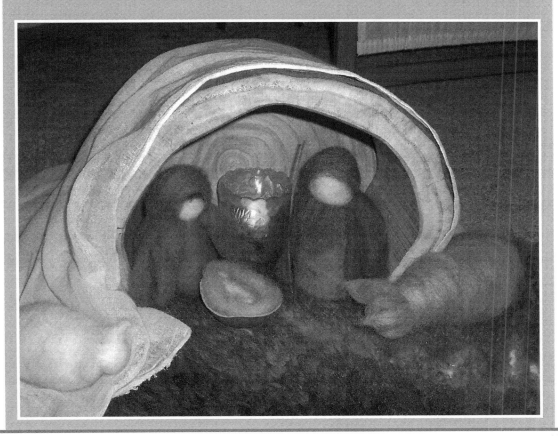

As awakeners of ancient memories, festivals turn our thoughts and feelings to the past.
But other thoughts also are aroused through the understanding of the content of these festivals,
thoughts that turn our eyes to the future of mankind,
which for us means the future of our souls.
Feelings are awakened which lend us the enthusiasm to live on into the future
and inspire our wills with strength so to work that we may grow
ever more and more adequate for our future tasks.

Rudolf Steiner, *The Festivals and Their Meaning*, 258.

When we think about the festival, we picture a point in time, a celebration of an acknowledged event. This may be a seasonal festival, a Christian or other cultural festival, or it may be our very own personal festival, the birthday. What does the word *festival* mean? It is a celebration, an acknowledgement of a remembered event, something of significance, an expression of joy and of life. In my work with infants and little children, I have broadened my understanding of this word *festival*.

Festivals in Daily Life

In a sense I experience each new day as a festival. Each time the table is prepared for a meal is a celebration, a festival of coming together socially, to partake of the food, lovingly prepared. This, one might say, has a quality of "communion" about it. The word *communion* encompasses a number of meanings; here I am talking about sharing, participating, a sense of fellowship.

This communion is elevated to the spiritual realm when one consciously acknowledges the way the food is grown, the nature spirits without which the food on our table would not exist, the good people who harvest the produce, the farm shop that sells us the vegetables, and the co-worker who takes the produce and transforms it, with the children, in the process of cooking.

This is supported by the table that becomes a festival table through careful setting of the places and the decoration that adorns it. This is a festival moment, and this we celebrate consciously every new day. Perhaps for many of us this is not conscious, and we need to awaken to what it can offer.

The festival realm brings with it an uplifting quality that lifts the moment out of the physical or earthly into the realm of the gods. Every time I consider the heavenly origins of the child, it is as if I speak directly to the child's angel. I am communing with the child's angel, thus forging a relationship with the child who is bathed in soul/spiritual warmth. The child experiences this relationship as a sense of well-being.

Festival Preparation

To be true in what we wish to bring to the child depends not so much on the wealth of possibilities[56] of what we could do but rather on our genuine relationship to any particular festival. We must immerse ourselves in the meaning of the festival if we are to convey a living experience to the child. We want the child to be touched by a gesture that brings the Christ into the moment, into the present when we live into the festival and its meaning. This applies to all our festivals.

This is the work of the adult. With very little children it is our inner work that carries the child and that creates the very atmosphere within the day nursery. It is the "breath of heaven" that we surround the child with. One works towards this, though not in the least expecting the little child to become involved in the way an older child would. We do need to understand and trust that this little child is involved very deeply. The consciousness with which we prepare the festival will penetrate the child right into her being, albeit unconsciously. Festivals with little children are living moments in time that the children experience and deeply connect with on a different level.

How we celebrate a particular festival will have much to do with our culture, with how our own early lives were fashioned. For some, these cultural celebrations are new, and a new relationship has to come about. For many today, for example, the birthday festival carries very little significance other than that the person is a year older.

It is important to note that there is no prescription or methodology for how we celebrate a festival, although there is tradition. I do not believe that the celebration of the festival lies so much in this realm of tradition, but rather it lives in the realm of living contemplation that brings an enlivening quality each time the festival is

---

56   Brigitte Barz, *Festivals with Children*, 8.

celebrated. This does not mean that we should be forever changing things. What it does mean is that each year, in our preparation for a particular festival, we will perceive it with new eyes. Through our study, new elements will come into play. This is a living study.

Inspiration comes from our preparation when each year we revisit what we did the previous year. With this revisiting we find the means of renewal, and doing this with a group of co-workers or colleagues can be a wonderful sharing and a real enlivening process for the festival preparation, and also for collegial working.

From a practical perspective we follow a cycle of planning, implementing, and reviewing. This is essential in all that we do in the working realm, be it a kindergarten or early childhood center. It is part of being responsible, of being ordered in our doing, of being prepared, of being one step ahead—which, when you have a group of around twenty little children, is essential for the well-being of both the children and the co-workers.

Planning gives a map, so to speak, a guide to what happened last year, a means to reflect. It is this map that will lead us into the renewal process for the coming year.

The reviewing of the festival time is as vital as the planning itself, for it is the review, the reflection on the festival, that will guide us in where we wish to take the festival in the following year.

The Festival Study

The planning begins with readings. These are appropriate pieces for study that are selected by the co-worker responsible for bringing the festival element to the pedagogical meeting. The reading is a meditative working and ideally begins at least three to four weeks prior to the festival. While we are engaging in the outer preparation with the children, we are engaged also in the inner preparation of our soul life that will enable a worthy gesture to permeate the day nursery with a living atmosphere.

During the four weeks prior to the festival, elements are worked with in the pedagogical meeting. This may be a reflection of what has been read or a group study. It will certainly include the songs we are going to sing. It may include our own personal questions that need to be discussed in a group. This can only happen where there is trust, where we have the confidence to say "I don't know."

In the Awhina pedagogical meeting, one half-hour is given to this festival study. This is ample time if each co-worker is engaged, both individually and collectively, and comes having already begun the preparation process.

Festivals and Nature

Any craft-making involved in the festival is usually done in the course of the day. This is but a gesture for the very young child, and if there is a festival gift to go home then this is generally for the little ones over two years of age.

While outer symbols are important because they bring helpful pictures to the child and to the family who may have had no previous connection to these happenings, what carries the most influence, what truly supports the child, is our inner preparation. We need to awaken to the inner experience of what the festival may offer and not become too dependent on what the outer world of nature is presenting. There is no doubt that the natural world lends support and nourishment, but we should not allow this to dominate our festival offering.

For example, let us look to the Easter season that culminates in the resurrection on Easter Sunday. In the northern hemisphere the long winter months are giving way to new beginnings and with it new growth, warmth, and color—a spring transition point. In the southern hemisphere there is at this time the transition to autumn, a colorful respite after the long hot days of summer.

A transition, a mediation, is experienced at this point of the year in the Easter festival—inner mediation that is outwardly expressed in the northern spring and in the southern autumn. No matter where we live in the world, we need to find an inner balance. This we can find in giving ourselves the time to take stock, to contemplate, to consider as we prepare for the festival.

A question that I have been working with for some time now is whether we rely too much on the season, or are we intent on finding a true inspiration in the essence and the meaning of the festival? I am talking here about the main festival points of the year. Do we try to make the festival fit the season, or do we allow the season to dictate the form of the festival? I offer this as food for thought, and a starting point for discussion.

If we ourselves want to understand what has occurred and if we make this experience our own in an enduring way, then the child will experience this through us. Our own attitude and our fulfillment create the festival for the child.

Planning for a Seasonal Motif—A Suggestion for Summer

The following thoughts are an example of how a festival or season may be brought to co-workers during a planning process.

The day nursery closes for its summer break from Christmas week for three weeks. The Three Kings Day celebrated on January 6th culminates the twelve holy nights that began with the birth of the Christ Child on December 25th and leads into the four weeks of Epiphany.

The word *epiphany* comes from the Greek word *epiphaneia*, which means "to shine above" or "to shine over." We return to Awhina in the height of summer, when the sun is at its hottest and the soul of the earth has expanded out into the cosmos.

Outwardly, the season reflects the heat of the sun. The garden is alive with the buzzing, busy bees, whose task of pollinating the flowers is indispensable in the life cycle of the plant and essential for the nutritional needs of the human being. Honey was our earliest sweet in Europe, used until Alexander the Great, returning from Asiatic exploration, brought with him the first sugar cane. Beeswax is just as ancient and was used in early times, as now, for candles as a medium of light.

We invite the bees inside in song and in verse, perhaps in activity; we bring them in through the light of the beeswax candle at morning tea. The golden colors of summer are reflected in the seasonal cloths and the colorful flowers of this season.

The following verse, written by Rudolf Steiner for children, beautifully captures the atmosphere of this time:

> Sunlight is flooding
> The widths of space.
> The song of the bird echoes
> Through the realms of the air.
> The blessing of plants sprouts
> From the being of earth.
> And human souls lift themselves
> In feelings of thankfulness
> To the spirits of the world.

Activities of summer days may include:

- Water, water and more water play; water counters the heat and reconnects the child with his or her spiritual origins[57]

- Watering of the garden, with longer deep soakings following morning play (when watering is brief and therefore shallow, which brings the roots of the plant to the surface)

- Bubble play

- Washing of sandpit toys in soapy water

- Fishing games in water

- Story time on a rug in a shady place in the garden

- Soapy water painting with buckets and wide brushes, particularly the stones and shells in the pathways

- Making walnut shell or leaf sailing boats

We each need to find our way into this time of the year and find possibilities to lead the child into an experience that is only possible at this season. As part of our planning, it is helpful to engage in a project that the child can experience as a real activity, connect him to the season, and that will engage his own will activity, as always, through imitating adults. Any project entered into needs to be carefully planned from all points of view and then should become part of every day for a period of time, in order for the children to live into the experience. An example might be to make walnut boats and then make a pond in which we can sail them.

Ask the question: What do I need? Gather all that you need so you do not have to remove yourself during your doing, which might include:

- A suitable basket to carry all bits and pieces

- Children's paintings to make into sails

- Glue, scissors, and sandpaper

---

57   Daniel Udo de Haes, *The Young Child*, 23.

Creating the boats might include:

- ▲ Preparing walnut shells, cleaning and sanding them beautifully

- ▲ Searching for little twigs, with the children, to hold the sail

- ▲ Cutting out sails

- ▲ Assembling the boats

The next steps would be:

- ▲ Prepare your pond. This could be a basin over which is draped a blue silk.

- ▲ Have a little verse or story to use as you sail the boats with the children

- ▲ Know that what you have prepared will work!

- ▲ Cleaning up should be part of your planning, as should tidying away the pond in readiness for the next time. How you tidy away is experienced by the child as much as anything you do.

- ▲ Wear an apron when you are engaged in any work.

It is preferable that any planning be brought first to the pedagogical meeting to share with colleagues, so that all have a picture of what is happening around the children and also to allow for suggestions from more experienced co-workers.

For ideas for activities, we often refer to the following books in the parent library:

Earthways, by Carol Petrash

All Year Round, by Ann Druit, Christine Fynes-Clinton, and Marije Rowling

Natural Childhood, by John B. Thomson

Festivals, Family and Food, by Diana Carey and Judy Large

Chapter 15
Research and Reflection

As Awhina developed, the creation of what I call "pedagogical papers" helped to form and define our practice. Because this way of working with very young children was new, I had to develop practices that spoke to the needs of very young children in care, bearing in mind that the co-workers mainly came from mainstream early childhood environments or training providers. The understanding of *why* and *how* needed to be clearly articulated from a "living" practical perspective.

When a particular paper was brought to the pedagogical meeting, this was used as advice and guidance but also as a working paper to be discussed and related to the daily practical work. It was expanded upon through sharing of personal experiences in a learning circle, the result of which was a heightened understanding through practical application.

The co-workers' insights came directly from the children, often when the smallest element of practice was changed. For example, when taking the time to slow one's gestures or movements, the co-worker would observe the response by the child. Sometimes this response would be in the gaze or in a smile from the child to the adult who had taken the time, indeed given the time, to the child.

When working in a way that is new and different, time is often needed to learn to observe in a way that enables the smallest nuances to be seen by the adult observer. While the nuances may be small, the impact on the child is huge when there is conscious acknowledgement (not necessarily of a verbal nature) of what is observed by the adult.

For example, the transition from the morning tea table to the bathroom can often be a time where chaos abounds and the noise level increases and some children may even dissolve into tears. However, with the most subtle of changes, this chaos and loudness can become a harmony of quiet and secure movement when two or three attentive caregivers remain seated at the table, "anchoring" and "holding" the children with a clear focus or ego presence.

The pedagogical paper is a valuable tool for developing the observation skills that lead to such healthy practices. This could be described as a "work in motion," developing a practice out of the experience of the day-to-day doing. The following examples are given as inspiration for developing your own research and reflection processes.

Planning an Environment from an Anthroposophical Perspective
The following is an example of a pedagogical paper, expanded upon for some weeks through explorative conversations.

Focus: to create an environment of creative doing, of real work where a wealth of opportunities and possibilities exist—opportunities that allow the young child to integrate into life.

The key for us as practitioners is twofold:

▲ Knowing the needs of the young child from a physical, emotional, and spiritual perspective

▲ Caring for, knowing, and managing the environment that surrounds the child in an empathetic way, allowing for the child to truly integrate into life in a meaningful way.

A good example could be the following: The fishing rods are carefully made and placed in the boat; however, just a short time later they are found with shells broken and the plaited lines pulled away from the rods. These rods need to be "taken hold of" again and lovingly repaired, preferably with and around the children, and placed back in the boat.

It is in the doing, the intention carried by the adult, that the child comes to learn about life. Perhaps the mending of the rods does not work the first time. Perhaps we need to make it our task to ensure that they are used in a right manner—a little story of a fishing trip, with everyone in the boat and repeated over three or four days, might lead to a more creative image for the children who may not have the experience of fishing. It is our striving, successful or otherwise, that the child experiences and connects with on an unconscious level.

When I plan an activity, I must ask the following questions:

▲ What is its value?

▲ Is it real, is it true, or am I in fact contriving something as a way of occupying the child?

I can plan only when I truly know the needs of the young child. I want to engage the child in a way that will support the child's incarnating/developmental journey. We are working with a moral and artistic education. We carry an inner picture, we pause, we endeavor to make each day richer for the quality of the etheric of the young child. We need to strive to be intelligent, meaningful, and "sensible," and the children will live into this. All that speaks to the child's senses has an effect. If the impressions are good, we support the healthy inner development of the child's physical body.

As an example of the preparatory work that can be done, these are some considerations when planning for the two-year-old and older child outdoors:

▲ Know the environment: what does the season ask for?

▲ What are the needs in the garden?

▲ What is being asked for in the care of the chickens?

▲ What needs to be mended? Mending is part of maintaining and one of the most important areas of consideration in the home environment.

▲ If digging is needed (for the children) and perhaps the sandpit is resting, find a suitable digging area. How do I make this activity worthwhile?

▲ Perhaps the boys do not want to "bake" in the sandpit; we need to observe what is not working and respond to the needs as they are led by the children.

▲ What did your own children like to do? Both boys and girls like to busy themselves in the sandpit, but do they always want to engage in the same type of play?

Boys connect strongly to the physical, the challenge and the joy of making things work, of doing. Provide possibilities such as planks of timber, boxes, tires, cable reels, short wooden ladders, pieces of rope, and so on.

- What can be achieved with some water, pipes, and sand is endless. However, we need to be able to enter into this doing with a real picture of the possibilities. We need to lead these young boys into the possibilities for creative play; pulley systems with buckets and ropes are a good beginning.

- Change the sandpit from time to time, remove some play/baking things, create something new, form a picture.

- We can only be engaged in our adult work when the child is likewise engaged; which comes first?

- Do I purposely bring out the wheelbarrows or do they sit in the garden shed, or is the child motivated through my activity to go and get a wheelbarrow?

Further questions and considerations that can help us create inner preparedness:

- Do I engage in picturing the children before I go to sleep?

- Do I know the needs of individual children?

- Am I fearful of those children who may appear difficult?

- Can I receive enough, be open enough to the children?

- An ego question: Have I lost my learning ability?

- Is there an imbalance between my home life and work life?

- Am I working with equanimity? Is there a balance between the polarities of sympathy and antipathy?

- Do I need to strengthen my ego forces?

Repetition is necessary for a strong and healthy etheric body, in order to transform later into forces of thinking. The children do the same things each day with a joy for life; this helps develop the memory. The child has a rhythmical rather than an abstract memory. The child before three years has a local memory: you show the child one thing and the child recalls the whole, in detail; the local memory gives the whole picture.

Early intellectualization results in the child not enjoying repetition and not being able to enter the healthy process of imitation. The child is a "clairvoyant" and does not need explanations; abstract thinking comes in through the process of imitation. The child, in imitating, does not exactly copy what we have done, but rather re-creates anew.

We, the adults, should endeavor to find a new quality every day. Through our inner effort we create a "presence." Out of an inner awareness we must endeavor to create each day afresh, out of the past.

The adult endeavors to cultivate an inner life of meditation. This helps strengthen the ego allowing a deeper penetration into the astral body. Engaging in artistic activity also supports this strengthening process. We, the adults, need to find the balance, not too much and not too little; this in turn supports ego activity in the young child.

Illness in the adult can be symptomatic of a lack of ego activity. We need to create a healthy organism. When the children experience this healthy, living organism, harmony exists; they will then know what to look for in later life. The adult can avoid "burn-out" through equilibrium of the ego.

We choose our situations in life. We have the possibility to identify with our destiny question in the work we choose, in the environment we find ourselves.

Children look at you, the adult, with love, and with this look they embrace the world.

Each preparation I enter into lightens or shares the load of my co-worker and prepares the way for the child.

This is being prepared in our work. This is planning for the day. This is planning for the child. This is working as part of a team.

Reflection on "Planning an Environment"
What follows is one of a number of reflections by co-workers on the topic.

I have chosen to focus on the idea that it is in the doing, the intention carried by the adult, that the child comes to learn about life, and that it is the striving, the follow-through, that engages the child.

Personally, I find this a real challenge. I have experienced many times how enormously my own sense of clear intention impacts on the behavior and well-being of the young child. On days when I am very clear and focused on my goal and follow through with it, the children are generally settled and engaged, be it with their own play or with helping me.

In contrast, on days where I move from one activity to the next in an aimless way, without a clear picture of my ultimate goal, the children are often unsettled and either having conflicts with each other or having avoidable accidents, as they are not feeling secure and embraced by a sense of purpose in the adult.

So, I truly understand the importance of clear intention and follow-through in integrating the child into life in a meaningful way. This leads to the question: Why is it so difficult to sustain a clear sense of intention and purpose in my work?

These really are destiny questions and seem to me to be closely related to the questions and statements about the ego: "Do I need to strengthen my ego forces?" "We regain ego forces by identifying more with what we are doing." "We choose our situations in life and we have the ability to identify with our destiny situation."

If I am clear about my overall goal or destiny in life, this strength of clarity and self-assurance will surely permeate all that I am and all that I do. The extent to which I have identified with my own destiny situation and strengthened my ego forces is the extent to which, on an everyday scale, I am able to follow through with tasks and carry them out in a meaningful way, rather than as aimless, piecemeal activities.

This sounds like a reasonable theory, but what am I to do with it? Obviously, performing my daily tasks can't wait until I have total clarity about my life purpose; this is the ongoing question of a lifetime. Again, it seems to me, that it is the conscious striving that is important here.

Even though it is impossible at my age (35) to have answered all my destiny questions, I can be conscious of what my values are and what principles I want to live by. Recently I committed myself to the goal of always striving towards being conscious of what is truly important, and constantly asking myself, "how much integrity do I have in giving priority to what really matters?"

In those pockets of time when my highest principles are in harmony with my actions, I feel purposeful, clear, and secure in who I am, and that I am working on "expanding." I feel so strongly how significantly more effective I am, when in that state, in supporting my co-workers and fulfilling my main task, which is to integrate the young child into life in a meaningful way. ▣

Chapter 16
Penetrating Our Practice Allows for Discernment

In order to reach the inner life of the child, we have to ask next in which way
does a child experience the world? Is his inner world entirely different?
A twofold answer is necessary for there are two separate phases of childhood.
The first phase extends to the moment when the child first says "I" to himself,
and the next phase is all the following period. This very moment in which the child suddenly realizes
"I am a self" is a most deeply felt experience for its inner life.
The German poet, Jean Paul, describes this moment remembered from his childhood by saying: "I
entered into the most sacred chamber of my innermost being."

Karl König, *Eternal Childhood*, 101.

It is my belief that we need to be aware of and awake to new perspectives on raising and caring for infants and young children. We can, however, only determine how and why we would introduce new practices when we have a thorough and penetrated knowledge of our own practice. We need to be able to articulate our practices in a way that speaks clearly to what we represent, in this case anthroposophical childcare.

Practices within any center, school, or organization are the tools through which our philosophy is expressed. When our work is well penetrated then the environmental sheaths that create the center or home are experienced in a living way, by the children in our care, by the parents who enter the environment, and by our colleagues working in the environment. When our practice is not clearly defined, however, when there is a lack of clear philosophical definition and understanding, then introducing new practices will simply add to this lack of definition and our very identity comes into question.

There are many approaches to childcare in the world today and we may find helpful ideas in some of them to the extent that such ideas resonate with and support the threefold understanding of the young child. An example is the work of Hungarian pediatrician Emmi Pikler. Her extensive research into the development of movement in the young child provides a wonderful tool, as does the gentle touch and respect that surrounds the young child during care routines developed by her in an orphanage setting. At the same time, one can also note that the need to foster the child's individuality at such a young age arose out of the orphanage situation. This is not necessary when children are able to be supported "into" life and cared for in an environment that works out of the threefold understanding of the human being.

I believe that our work from an anthroposophical perspective embracing body, soul and spirit needs to become more penetrated and more visible, if we are to allow the spiritual entity of the young child to fully incarnate in a healthy way. For me personally this is the gift that I received from attending the Pikler Institute: a greater awareness of the need to make anthroposophical practice more visible in the world.

Anthroposophical childcare is itself like a newborn infant, a *Taonga* (a Maori word meaning "a precious gift") that has been quietly nurtured and breathed with warming life, its potential seen by only a few. Now it is time to unfold the nurturing wrap and allow the world to experience this gift, so that its light can shine for infants and little children and for the life of the family in today's modern world.

Let us look at the anthroposophical perspective and what it means to work out of such a background.

▲ The child's incarnating journey is one of being caressed rather than being pushed or directed into life. We could bring an imagination similar to the process of the butterfly emerging from the chrysalis, the warmth of the sun being akin to the ego warmth emanating from the attentive caregiver.

▲ The child is a being of body, soul, and spirit, and all that involves the child is done with an understanding of this threefoldness.[58]

▲ Rather than promoting early independence, the adult surrounds the child with an empathetic soul gesture which acknowledges her spiritual entity and which allows her to reach an independence of being in her own time, at her own pace. This is acknowledging the unique individuality of the human being with the highest respect.

▲ The adult "carries" the child, a conscious ego activity which allows the child to dream into, to be at one with, the physical world.

---

58   Edmond Schoorel, *The First Seven Years*, 15ff.

▲ It is not until two-and-a-half to three years of age that a "second birth," which one could call the true birth, takes place. This is when the child says "I" to himself. Around this time the child begins to experience himself more independently. Until this time, the child lives within the etheric and soul realm of his parent and primary caregiver. He experiences this "holding mantle" as a sheath of warming well-being.

▲ The child is entirely a sense organ.[59] All that surrounds the child, in the broadest sense, is absorbed by the child, working on the incomplete inner organs. The child has no means to discriminate. It is the adult's responsibility to filter these sense impressions for the child. One could say that the adult forms a cocoon around the child, the layers folding back little by little, allowing the child to experience that which she is becoming more ready to meet.

▲ The child is not asked to make choices. He is, in fact, as yet not capable of making a choice; the young child's brain has not developed enough. Rather, the choice is made on behalf of the child by the adult whose responsibility it is to guide and protect as the child awakens to the world. This is respecting the child on his path of "becoming," as an entity of body, soul, and spirit.

▲ During these first years the little child is in constant movement between the physical world and the world of spirit. This "mode" of the young child is often referred to as a mono- or dream consciousness.[60] It is the role of the adult to maintain the possibility for this consciousness by not "awakening" the little one too soon or too abruptly and by surrounding him with beauty, with true and healthy images of the physical environment. By allowing the child to breathe in through the senses all that the environment offers, we are respecting the child and his spiritual origin.

▲ The child at this age is a "being of the will" in constant physical movement. We allow this will activity to reach its potential by not only allowing the child the space to move, but by allowing the child to move forward in all that he does, at his own pace, in his own time.

---

59   Rudolf Steiner, *Understanding Young Children*, 86.
60   Ibid, 46.

▲   Self education[61] is the priority when working with the very young child. We, the adults, are the foundation stone for the child. We need to be able to stand before the child with sincerity and integrity. We need to know who we are. We need to be sincere in how we represent ourselves to the child. We are prepared to enter into this self-development for the sake of the child, as well as for our own inner development, knowing that everything in the environment in its broadest sense will influence the child for the whole of life.

▲   During the first seven years learning through imitation is an integral part of childhood. The adult must be worthy of this imitation.

▲   Our communication with the infant, with the child, is a communication based on language, quietly spoken and often sung. It is also a language of gesture and loving communication that creates an embrace: by touch, by stroking, through thoughtful intention and warming heart forces. When we engage the heart forces, the realm of communication expressed through gesture is lifted into the realm of spirit. The communication becomes a spiritual communication. A foundation of trust develops; a relationship is formed. It is this world of gesture that surrounds the child at all times. The young child lives and breathes within this realm of warmth which emanates from the adult as a mantle of threefoldness—of the body through touch, of the soul in warm objectivity, and of the spirit in communion with the child's angel.

▲   Rudolf Steiner once said, "Our aim is not to touch the spirit but to let it be awakened."[62] This, one could describe as the carrying motif in our working with the infant and young child. Through our consciousness, through a right gesture, we allow the spirit to be awakened in the young child.

▲   Children who live in an environment of warmth and love and good example are children living in their proper element,[63] able to be truly in the mode of childhood, to move freely and to play freely. Warmth, love and good example do not just happen but need to be arrived at through a conscious working, through a conscious preparation that includes the environment in its broadest sense.

---

61   Rudolf Steiner, *Understanding Young Children*, 3.
62   Ibid, 43.
63   Rudolf Steiner, *The Education of the Child*, 22.

▲ It is an indisputable fact that the rightful place to raise and nurture a child is the home. The archetypal home is that space which enfolds the child with living sheaths that support the child into life. In the work of the day nursery, the archetypal home is emulated, through a conscious working with the fourfold sheaths, with particular attention to those activities that live in the domestic realm.[64]

▲ Nutrition[65] is an intrinsic element of an anthroposophical practice. This includes the relationship of the plant to the human being in terms of threefoldness. The root (where the mineralizing process occurs) supports the sense-nerve system, the thinking; the leaves (the breathing organ of plants) support the rhythmical system, the feeling, the heart and blood circulation; the fruit and flower (metabolic and reproductive forces) support primarily the metabolic system. The grains, even though primarily fruit, have all three spheres combined in them, even mineralizing forces, normally only found in the root of a plant. This is the secret of the grains. The need to use biodynamically grown grain, so that we can obtain the most nutritional value when building up our own etheric or life forces, stands in the realm of self-care as well as self-education.

This by no means covers all aspects of an anthroposophical approach to the care of the very young child but rather prepares a foundation. We need to draw our inspiration from Rudolf Steiner's view of the young child, and stand behind the practices we develop thereby.

Many practices that are intrinsic to an anthroposophical perspective when we are embracing care of infants and very young children are not widely known. This is new work in the world. We need to redefine the inspiration that Anthroposophy can and does bring to this important work. Indeed, this is the task in our present time, to make these practices more visible. ▣

---

64   Audrey E. McAllen, *Sleep*, 26.

65   Michaela Glöckler, *A Guide to Child Health*, 246.

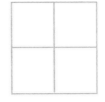

Afterword:
A Mother's Story

Janet Metelerkamp

Father and mother provide the first and all-important relationships which the child forms, so that his destiny may unfold. In the growing process of the child, the father has the same importance as the mother. However everything that seems easy for the mother, bearing the mark of the immediacy of care and love, seems more difficult for the father. His relationship to the child entails an ever-renewed decision. The mother opens the path into the world by creating a space around the child in which the threats of darkness, fear and anxiety are stilled and calmed. The task of the father is different: he has to appear before the child as an example. In observing small children, we can notice how they stand and walk like their father, his attitudes and postures are imitated by the little son or little daughter. Imitation characterizes the father-relationship; trust characterizes the relationship to the mother.

Karl König, Eternal Childhood, 95.

I was eight months pregnant when we started to consider what we would do when I returned to work after having our first baby. I had a year's parental leave ahead of me, but the prospect of entrusting my child to other people's care filled me with terror. A work colleague suggested we look at Awhina: "The food's great, all organic, AND you just want to spend all day in the garden," he said.

My daycare terror only became more acute once our precious Joshua was born. Joshua was three to four months old when I started making enquiries by telephone. I called three centers and a nanny service before calling Awhina. The initial calls did nothing to allay my fears. The responses were curt, with caregivers sounding hassled or stressed and unenthusiastic about the prospect of my beautiful precious baby being placed in their care. And the background noise was not encouraging. It was not harmonious.

Next I called Awhina. The person I spoke with was calm and reassuring and the background noise was made by busy, happy children. The suggestion was that I come into the garden and see if Awhina was for us. Joshua was about five months old when we started to make our tentative pilgrimages into the garden. On the very first day we entered through the gate, the garden enveloped us and drew us in, welcoming us "home," as it were. The natural environment and manner in which the caregivers interacted with the children, even when dealing with "unacceptable" behaviors, was so positive. My soul had found a safe haven and my terror evaporated.

With every visit to Awhina I became more relaxed, feeling safer and more at home. Joshua loved sitting in the garden with the children playing around him and coming up to us. His happiness in the garden was the sign to me that this was the right and only choice. With my second baby, Rebekah, it feels natural that she should join Joshua at Awhina. I am blessed that this time there is no fear and concern at finding the right place.

Why is Awhina different? The main differences are intangible. They are in the caregivers, in their dedication and the love they have for the children. They are in the positivity and nurturing way with which they do everything, from the mundane to the fundamental; how they deal with and nurture the children through their different phases and life experiences. They are in the unspoken rituals and communications that invite one into Awhina, the way in which we the parents are accepted, supported, and encouraged. It is our "other home" too, as we leave a huge part of ourselves with our babies when we go.

A core difference at Awhina is the way in which children are allowed to just be, to evolve through play, at their own pace. There is none of the achieving-of-milestones-by-certain-ages approach. The evolution of the children in an essentially natural environment through the garden, the chickens, the use of organic and biodynamically grown foods, the seasonally related rituals, playthings made from natural materials, their involvement in daily life, all provide the most unadulterated, "whole" introduction to the world. This in itself is a major achievement in a technologically contaminated and rushed society.

Awhina is also a support for the family. The support we received began long before Joshua actually started at Awhina. When he was six months old, we traveled to South Africa to visit family. Prior to leaving we had been making regular visits to the garden, and it was known that we were going on our trip. At the last visit we were presented with Joshua's first dolly, his sleeping dolly, to take with us to keep as something constant over what would be six weeks of upheaval and staying at five different places. In addition we were given advice on a jetlag remedy from Weleda. This remedy reduced my jetlag from seven days to two, relative to previous experience. With a six-month-old baby this was a godsend.

Once we returned from the trip, we had a phase-in period to Awhina for. The transition was adapted based on the caregivers' observations of Joshua's settling in. Since then, there have been innumerable instances of Awhina's complete dependability and positive influence on our lives. When Bruce (my husband) was hospitalized with a back injury, Awhina stepped in, with Josh's godparents, as my primary backup and support. I did not have to worry about Josh at all as I could completely trust in the care he was receiving. This was very reassuring without having any other family in New Zealand.

During my second pregnancy I was given wonderful, sound advice on how it would impact Joshua, and how to handle this. I met the Awhina mother/child nurse at an Awhina workshop and went to her for rhythmical massage prior to giving birth. I also went to Awhina's cranial osteopath. These latter two elements, I believe, were fundamental to a very positive birth experience with Rebekah, as compared with Joshua's, which was fraught with intervention.

Rebekah is now almost eight months old and about to start one day a week at Awhina. Prior to and since her birth we have experienced a considerable amount of upheaval, with family visiting from South Africa, the changes around the household, and our adjustment to being parents of two children. The impact on Joshua and me has been considerable. These have been very difficult to handle at times, with my lamenting the loss of my sweet baby boy, and the arrival of a fearful, unhappy, and clingy toddler in his place. My own state of mind has not been constructive either. The support for Joshua and me through this phase has been incredibly nurturing.

These transitions I experience as much as my child. With the sound advice, there when I need it, the happy child has again emerged, and so has a calmer mum and hence a happy household.

The Awhina library has been a wonderful resource for books on child development and motherhood. These have provided me with insight and ideas and, perhaps more importantly, affirmation of feelings and senses for me as a mother. Awhina is the place we go for advice, ideas, and guidance on all manner of things from toilet training to education. We always come away with new confidence and positivity, to continue on with this role of parent—the most challenging and rewarding endeavor we have attempted, and the most significant achievement of our lives.

We try to bring Awhina ways into the home. Above all else, we retain the daily rhythm. We guard it jealously as it forms the backbone of a stable, happy day for us. The daily rhythm includes meals together as a family, quiet time, indoor playtime, and outdoor playtime. Another gleaning from the ways of Awhina is the involvement of the children in daily household tasks as part of their play, to make it as natural a happening as playing in the sandpit. Joshua loves to be involved with all things, from washing dishes and hanging washing to cooking and baking. He even enjoys mopping and dusting! Gardening is another favorite pastime.

We attempt to avoid the use of negative language like "no" or "don't." With Awhina's guidance we approach these situations with "we do" or "we may," or we use diversion. We use natural materials wherever possible, in clothing and in playthings, and the children love to collect all manner of things from the garden and beach for their play. We now use Weleda remedies for everyday bumps and spills and other ailments that seem to be part of children's lives at this age. The sleeping dollies are an integral part of the children's bedtime; just as the singing of nursery rhymes have become constant in our life now. I didn't use to sing and now I do—a little flat and off-key, but I sing!

We have tried to draw on the seasonal rituals that are part of Awhina, and have tried to create some of our own. For example, bulb planting has become a big part of our Easter holidays, and when the Easter basket comes home from Awhina, we plan and then plant our bulbs together. I write this looking out at daffodils, tulips, and freesias planted last Easter with Joshua. We also weave baskets of willow to take gifts of Easter eggs to special friends and the children's godparents. Prior to Christmas we have adopted the Advent ritual of opening the Advent calendar together. On Christmas Eve, we walk down our road and take a small gift to neighbors and wish them well.

Awhina is the first place that I have felt completely accepted and unjudged, where my differences in belief and values from mainstream society are actually considered quite normal. As these are unconsciously transferred from me to my children, it is incredibly important that they feel respected, valued, and acknowledged as individuals. The Awhina approach is a healthy, wholesome influence on our lives. It is such an essential alternative to the frenetic consumerist world we live in today, allowing us to connect with our children, our souls, and ourselves. We feel we are better parents because of Awhina. 🏠

Janet Metelerkamp was born in the late 1960s in a remote, mountainous part of South Africa and grew up on a family farm which bordered on the Kingdom of Lesotho. She later worked in a Biotechnology research laboratory in Dusseldorf, Germany and traveled around Europe and Turkey. She returned to South Africa for more travel and work in the manufacturing industry. In 1997, she and her husband immigrated to New Zealand to start a new life together and in 2002 began the most exciting life experience of all: parenthood. Her most precious blessings and greatest achievements are Joshua and Rebekah.

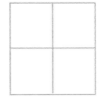

References

Carey, Diana, and Judy Large. *Festivals, Family and Food*. Stroud, UK: Hawthorn Press, 1982.

De Haes, Daniel Udo. *The Young Child: Creative Living with Two to Four Year Olds*. Edinburgh: Floris Books, 1986.

Druit, Ann, Christine Fynes-Clinton, and Marije Rowling. *All Year Round*. Stroud, UK: Hawthorn Press, 1997.

Education (Early Childhood) Regulations 1998. Published under the authority of the New Zealand Government.

Fancourt, Robin. *Brainy Babies*. Auckland: Penguin Books (NZ) Ltd., 2000.

Gerber, Magda. *Your Self Confident Baby*. New York: John Wiley & Sons, Inc., 1998.

Glöckler, Michaela. *A Guide to Child Health*. Edinburgh: Floris Books, 1990.

Grimm, Ruediger. "The Essence of Social Therapy." *Journal of Curative Education and Social Therapy*. New Year, 2003.

Helliwell, Tanis. *Summer with the Leprechauns*. Nevada City, CA: Blue Dolphin Publishing, Inc., 1997.

König, Karl. *Eternal Childhood*. North Yorkshire, UK: Camphill Press, Botton Village, 1994.

Kühne, Petra. *Säuglingsernährung*. Bad Vilbel: Arbeitskreis fuer Ernaehrungsforschung e.V., 2002.

Lillico, Dorothy H. "That Other Self." *Perspectives*. Dec. 1993 – Jan. 1994.

McAllen, Audrey E. *Sleep*. Fair Oaks, CA: Rudolf Steiner College Press, 2004.

Pere, Rosemarie. *Ako: Concepts and Learning in the Maori Tradition*. Hamilton, New Zealand: University of Waikato, 1982.

Perry, Bruce. "Childhood Experience and the Expression of Genetic Potential: What Childhood Neglect Tells Us About Nature and Nurture." In *Brain and Mind*, Volume 3, No. 1, 2002.

Petrash, Carol. *Earthways*. Mt. Rainier, MD: Gryphon House, 1992.

Ropiha, Awhitia. "The Four Cornerstones of Health as Related to Awhina." Professional development workshop presented at Awhina Day Nursery, Havelock North, New Zealand, March 18, 2000.

Salter, Joan. *The Incarnating Child*. Stroud, UK: Hawthorn Press, 1987.

Schoorel, Edmond. *The First Seven Years*. Fair Oaks, CA: Rudolf Steiner College Press, 2004.

Sensory Awareness Foundation, *Bulletin*. Number 14, Winter 1994.

Steiner, Rudolf. *Calendar of the Soul*. Forest Row, UK: Temple Lodge Publishing, 2004.

———. *Nutrition and Health: Two Lectures to Workmen*. London: Rudolf Steiner Press, undated booklet (lectures given in 1924).

———. *The Education of the Child.* New York: Anthroposophic Press, 1996.

———. *The Festivals and Their Meaning.* London: Rudolf Steiner Press, 1981.

———. *Knowledge of the Higher Worlds.* New York: Anthroposophic Press, 1947.

———. *Understanding Young Children: The Child Before the Seventh Year.* Stuttgart, Germany: International Association of Waldorf Kindergartens, 1975.

———. *Verses and Meditations.* London: Rudolf Steiner Press, 1979.

Te Whaariki. Early Childhood Curriculum. Wellington New Zealand: Learning Media Ltd., 1996.

Thomson, John B. *Natural Childhood.* London: Gaia Books Ltd., 1994.

Van Duin, Veronica. *Homemaking as a Social Art.* London: Rudolf Steiner Press, 2000.

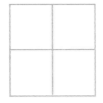

Suggestions for Further Reading

Brazelton, T. Berry And Stanley I. Greenspan. *The Irreducible Needs Of Children.* Cambridge, MA: Da Capo Press, Perseus Books Group, 2000.

Goddard Blythe, Sally. *The Well Balanced Child.* Stroud, UK: Hawthorn Press, 2004.

Jenkinson, Sally. *The Genius Of Play.* Stroud, UK: Hawthorn Press, 2001.

Koehler, Dr. Henning. *Working With Anxious, Nervous and Depressed Children.* Fair Oaks, CA: Association Of Waldorf Schools Of North America, 2001.

Large, Martin. *Who Is Bringing Them Up?* Gloucester, UK: Self-published, 1980.

Lievegoed, Bernard. *The Eye Of The Needle.* Stroud, UK: Hawthorn Press, 1993.

———. *The Battle For The Soul.* Stroud, UK: Hawthorn Press, 1994.

McAllen, Audrey E. *Reading Children's Drawings.* Fair Oaks, CA: Rudolf Steiner College Press, 2004.

Scheffer, Mechthild. *Bach Flower Therapy.* London: Thorsons Publishing Group, 1990.

Soper, John. *Bio-dynamic Gardening*. Clent, UK: Biodynamic Agricultural Association, 1983.

Steiner, Rudolf. *Anthroposophy in Everyday Life*. Hudson, NY: Anthroposophic Press, 1995.

———. *Man As Symphony of the Creative Word*. London: Rudolf Steiner Press, 1978.

Van Houten, Coenraad. *Awakening The Will*. Forest Row, UK: Temple Lodge Publishing, 2003.

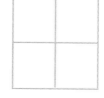

Appendix A
The Day Book

The day book is a tool for communication. It is what the caregiver greeting the parent in the morning uses to record relevant information about the child's previous night. It also serves as a focal point for the daily management practices at Awhina and records the following:

- The child's well-being in transition from home to Awhina, including how the child slept and when he awoke

- Medications, both homeopathic and allopathic, that the child may be required to have (see medication chart)

- Messages, relevant to children/parents and caregivers

- Notification of equipment that needs mending or general required maintenance

- Nursery checks on sleeping babies (to be conducted every ten minutes)—each tick represents ten minutes with each half hour written in. When an infant is unwell with a cough, cold, or general breathing discomfort, then the caregiver is to physically check the child.

- Daily menus

- Bed linen wash for part-time children, every other week

- Bed linen wash for full-time children, weekly

- Room (air) temperature in winter months, weekly

- Water temperature, kitchen and bathroom, monthly

All accidents and mishaps are written up in the accident register found in the first aid drawer. All co-workers are expected to read the day book on arrival in the morning as well as reconnecting with it mid-morning, mid-day, and mid-afternoon.

Appendix B
Equipment
in the Awhina Garden

This list includes all that lives in the garden—both conventional and perhaps more unconventional equipment.

▲ The garden gate

▲ Meandering pathways into which have been placed smooth stones and shells

▲ Surfaces that include concrete, sand, earth, bark, grass, and bricks

▲ A stone path garden with river stones of different shapes and sizes

▲ A gently sloping slide as part of what is called the slide-house, integrating wooden climbing steps

▲ Digging areas: an earth area; a large sandpit surrounded with flowers, shrubs, and trees; and a smaller sandpit enfolded with a wooden surround for the little children

▲ Pathways bordered with various herbs and scent-filled plants

▲ A boat for fishing

▲ The garden shed with spades, extra buckets, planks of wood, boxes, planting trays and pots, and all manner of bits and pieces needing to be tidied away

▲ Logs of all description and sizes, used for climbing, trains, and so on, and as tables

- ▲ Trees to offer fruit, shade, flowers, and beautiful leaves in the autumn, and one or two for climbing

- ▲ Two swings: a wooden horse swing and a tire swing

- ▲ Wooden wagons (for pulling along) and wooden wheelbarrows

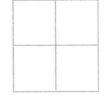

Appendix C
The Awhina Healing Basket

The Awhina Healing Basket contains Weleda remedies as well as the usual first aid requisites:

- Bandages
- Cotton wool
- Band-aids
- Scissors, tweezers, safety pins, stainless steel bowl, eye bath
- Thermometer
- Accident register
- Disposable gloves
- First aid manual
- Disinfectant (kept in laundry room)
- Remedies used:

    Bruising, sprains and strains:
    Weleda Arnica cream (do not apply to broken skin)

Burns, insect bites and stings:
Weleda Combudoron lotion; cool burns with a solution of Combudoron and water—then apply Combudoron gel

Cuts, grazes and wounds:
To clean wounds, use Weleda Hypercal lotion, then apply Hypercal cream, especially for grazes

Weleda Calendula healing cream for cuts (the wound must be clean)

Oral remedies for physical and emotional shock and trauma after injuries and accidents:
Weleda Arnica 6x or Weleda arnica pilules

Breathing difficulties caused by a heavy cold:
Weleda plantago eucalyptus chest rub and catarrh cream

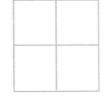

Appendix D
Demeter and Biodynamics

Demeter International and its national member organizations certify biodynamic food and products in over fifty countries.

Biodynamic agriculture is a method of organic farming and home gardening that treats the farm or garden as an individual organism, emphasizing the holistic development and interrelationship of the soil, plants, and animals as a closed, self-nourishing system.

Biodynamic farming and gardening emphasizes the use of manures and composts and the exclusion of the use of artificial chemicals. Methods unique to the biodynamic approach include the use of special preparations as compost additives and sprays, and the use of an astrological calendar to determine times of planting and harvesting. Biodynamic agriculture has its basis in Anthroposophy, founded by Rudolf Steiner.

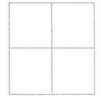

Appendix E
Food Group Sources

Protein: grains, dairy products, nuts. For older children over three years of age: meat and fish, eggs, legumes.

Fats: grains, nuts and seeds, dairy products, oils (organic and cold pressed, not processed—best are olive, safflower, and sunflower), avocados, green leafy vegetables. For older children: meat.

Carbohydrates: grains, dates, raisins, unrefined sugar, potatoes, and honey. It is preferable to eat starches that break down into sugar rather than eating straight sugar.

Minerals: grains, vegetables, herbs, milk, salt. In the first twelve months there should be no salt added to the child's diet. Even later too much salt in the first years stresses the heart and circulatory system. This can lead to high blood pressure in early years. Only in puberty or even later is the need for salt similar to that of the adult.

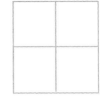

Appendix F
The Eightfold Path

Adapted by Bernadette Raichle from Rudolf Steiner,
Knowledge of the Higher Worlds
(New York: Anthroposophic Press, 1947, p. 137ff).

This series of daily meditations is available for co-workers, who each read them quietly before the day with the children begins.

Sunday
Right Judgment

Determine or decide on even the most insignificant matter only after fully reasoned deliberation. All unthinking behavior, all meaningless actions should be kept away from the soul.

Have well-weighed reasons for everything. Abstain from doing anything for which there is no significant reason.

When one is convinced of the rightness of the decision, hold fast to it with inner steadfastness.

Monday
Right Word

Only what has sense and meaning should come from the lips of one striving for higher development. Talking for the sake of talking—to fill in time—is in this sense harmful.

Disjointed kinds of conversation and meaningless remarks should be avoided. This does not mean shutting oneself off, but rather leading the conversation to significance. One adopts a thoughtful attitude to conversation, taking all aspects into account.

Never talk without cause—rather, be gladly silent. One tries not to talk too much or too little.

First listen quietly; then reflect on what has been said.

Tuesday
Right Deed

Actions should not be disturbing to others. When one needs to act, then one should deliberate carefully how one can best meet the occasion, for the good of the whole.

When one does things out of one's own initiative, consider most thoroughly beforehand the effect of one's actions on all else.

Wednesday
Right Standpoint

Live in harmony with nature and with spirit.

External trivialities of life should be avoided, as should anything that brings unrest and haste into one's life. Hurry over nothing, but do not be indolent.

Look on life as a means to improve oneself and as a means to higher development. Be on time.

Thursday
Right Habit

One should take care to do nothing that lies beyond one's powers, but also to leave nothing undone that lies within them.

Look beyond the everyday and set for oneself aims and ideals connected with the highest duties of a human being.

For instance, try to make these exercises more conscious, for you and for others that you may help or advise in the future.

Let these exercises become a conscious habit.

Friday
Right Memory

Endeavor to learn as much as possible from life.

All that comes to us gives us the opportunity to learn more from life. If one has done something inadequately, this becomes a motive for doing better the next time.

Likewise when we see others in the same situation, we observe them with a like end in view—with love and not with judgment.

One uses past experiences to assist with one's decisions and achievements.

One can learn something from everyone—even from children, if one is attentive.

Saturday
Right Opinion

Pay attention to your ideas. Think only significant thoughts.

Learn little by little to separate the essential from the nonessential, the eternal from the transitory, truth from mere opinion.

In listening to the other, try to be inwardly still, foregoing all judgment even in one's thoughts and feelings.

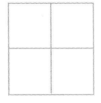

Appendix G
Self-Care

A sevenfold way to practice the development
of a free and lively approach to daily life
From *Homemaking as a Social Art*, by Veronica Van Duin
(London: Rudolf Steiner Press, 2000, p. 125ff)

1   The first thing to aim for is good physical health. This means healthy eating, so that less illness will occur. When illness does arise, using medicines that reinforce etheric activity is the wisest choice. Sleeping enough, taking exercise, finding rhythm in daily life, allowing things to happen peacefully are all part of this first step.

2   The second step is to recognize one's place as a member of the human race. Each individual is no better or worse that the other. This means that what happens anywhere in the world is as much part of one's life experience as are the things that happen at home. This attitude encourages compassion and empathy for all human beings and brings in its wake warmth of soul. Patience with people's oddities will also be one of its side effects.

3   The third step is to acknowledge the fact that whatever one thinks actually touches the object of one's thoughts as much as a physical blow or caress. The fact that thoughts have power can be used as a force for good. Sending positive thoughts into the world, to people who suffer, as well as to those one loves, and to those with whom one may find it difficult to live, can bring very satisfactory rewards. Sleep becomes wholesome and refreshing if one's thoughts have the wings of love to bear them. Moreover, many knotty problems in daily life can develop positive results when good thoughts are offered to their cause.

4   The fourth step is to acknowledge oneself as a valid and effective individual spirit. Holding fast to the conviction that the center of consciousness is within one's own soul provides a very firm anchor in the stormy sea of life. Self-confidence grows with the certainty of knowing the self. Knowing the self means to accept not only one's gifts, but also one's failures. To be human means to be imperfect and yet have the desire to reach for perfection. Loving the self makes it possible to love others, because in their weaknesses we recognize a common bond.

5   The fifth step requires an adherence to resolutions made until a new resolution is taken, or a decisive alteration is made. To be able to hold fast to one's decisions, and yet have the greatness of soul to change direction if necessary, means that balance and flexibility can be practiced creatively and without losing one's direction. This makes the fears and uncertainty of daily life recede, because one will be creating one's own unique mission statement.

6   The sixth step is to experience gratitude for all living things, for life itself and for the world around us. Gratitude is an attitude of soul, rather than an action, and so paves the way for growth and change. It opens doors and overcomes barriers between people. Acknowledging each other's efforts makes daily life so very much more pleasant.

7   The seventh step is to recognize that these attitudes of soul enrich the spirit. By trying to live in this sevenfold way, the faculty of being in the right place at the right time will be just one of the tangible outcomes. The balance that all homemakers seek as being essential to their task can become as natural as breathing.

Wonder

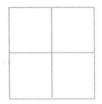

How like___ an an - gel came I down! How bright are all_____ things here! When first a - mong his works I did ap - pear, Oh, how their glor - ry___ me did crown!